Secrets of Awesome Dinner Guests:

What Walt Disney, Steve Jobs, Oprah Winfrey, Albert Einstein, Martin Luther King, Jr., Helen Keller, and John Lasseter Can Teach You About Success, Power Communication and Fulfillment

(The Power of Your Personal Brand)

2nd Edition*

Tom Marcoux

America's Communication Coach

TFG Thought Leader

Speaker-Author of 23 books

Blogger, BeHeardandBeTrusted.com

A QuickBreakthrough Publishing Edition

* edition with significant additions; formerly titled *Darkest Secrets of Business Communication*

ISBN: 0615975399
ISBN-13: 978-0615975399

QuickBreakthrough Publishing is an imprint of Tom Marcoux Media, LLC. More copies are available from the publisher, Tom Marcoux Media, LLC. Please call (415) 572-6609 or write TomSuperCoach@gmail.com

or visit www.TomSuperCoach.com

or Tom's blog: www.BeHeardandBeTrusted.com

This book was developed and written with care. Names and details were modified to respect privacy.

Disclaimer: The author and publisher acknowledge that each person's situation is unique, and that readers have full responsibility to seek consultations with health, financial, spiritual and legal professionals. The author and publisher make no representations or warranties of any kind, and the author and publisher shall not be liable for any special, consequential or exemplary damages resulting, in whole or in part, from the reader's use of, or reliance upon, this material.:

Other Books by Tom Marcoux:

- Be Heard and Be Trusted: How to Get What You Want
- Nothing Can Stop You This Year!
- Darkest Secrets of Persuasion and Seduction Masters
- Darkest Secrets of Charisma
- Darkest Secrets of Negotiation Masters
- Darkest Secrets of the Film and Television Industry Every Actor Should Know
- Darkest Secrets of Making a Pitch to the Film and Television Industry
- Darkest Secrets of Film Directing
- Darkest Secrets of Small Business Marketing

Praise for *Secrets of Awesome Dinner Guests:*

"This book helps you avoid communication traps that can hamper your business success. It also helps you to build a powerful personal brand that will inspire people to offer you great opportunities." – Danek S. Kaus, author of *You Can Be Famous: Insider Secrets to Getting Free Publicity*

"This book will increase your business success. Communication is the key. Tom shows you how to create an effective personal brand. I've hired Tom as my media coach and his strategies gain great results. " – Dr. JoAnn Dahlkoetter, author of *Your Performing Edge* and coach to CEOs and Olympic Gold Medalists

Praise for Tom Marcoux's Other Work

"*Create Your Best Life* is an uplifting and practical book. You'll learn skills in persuasion, charisma, confidence, influence and emotional strength — all vital elements to help you positively change the world. To make a dream come true, you'll need to get people enrolled in your vision. This is *the book* that helps you get great things done!" – Dr. JoAnn Dahlkoetter, author of *Your Performing Edge* and coach to CEOs and Olympic Gold Medalists

"In *Darkest Secrets of Persuasion and Seduction Masters*, learn useful countermeasures to protect you from being darkly manipulated."
– David Barron, co-author, *Power Persuasion*

"In *Be Heard and Be Trusted*, Tom's advice on how to remain true to yourself and establish authentic rapport with clients is both insightful and reality based. He [shows how] to establish oneself as a credible expert." -Arthur P. Ciaramicoli, Ed.D., Ph.D., author *The Curse of the Capable*, and *The Power of Empathy*

"*Nothing Can Stop You This Year* is a treasure trove of tips, tools, and terrific ideas—practical, reassuring, and energizing! Tom provides wonderful resources for achieving your goals." – Elayne Savage, Ph.D., author of *Don't Take It Personally! The Art of Dealing with Rejection*

Visit Tom's blog: www.BeHeardandBeTrusted.com

CONTENTS

DEDICATION AND ACKNOWLEDGEMENTS

This book is dedicated to the terrific book and film consultant, and author Johanna E. Mac Leod. It is also dedicated to the other team members. Thanks to David MacDowell, Sherry Lusk and Joan Harrison for editing. Thanks to my father, Al Marcoux, for his concern and efforts for me. Thanks to my mother, Sumiyo Marcoux, a kind, generous soul. Thanks to Johanna E. Mac Leod for rendering this book's front and back cover. Thank you to Higher Power. Thanks to our readers, audiences, clients, my graduate/college students and my team members of Tom Marcoux Media, LLC. The best to you.

BOOK ONE:
SECRETS OF BUSINESS COMMUNICATION (AND YOUR COUNTERMEASURES)

Imagine you could have dinner with some extraordinary people who like you and want to support you! What an amazing conversation you'd participate in. Oprah Winfrey said, *"Surround yourself with only people who are going to lift you higher."*

I never expected to write this book but something surprised me. I was moved by real positive responses that graced a video I produced and posted on Facebook. In the video, I talked of *Walt Disney's Strategy for Success* which enhanced the innovative Disneyland.

From such positive responses to the video, I then thought about what it takes to make our dreams come true. It really helps to talk with *people who accomplished what you want to do.* Unfortunately, like weeds, energy-draining opinions surround us. I've seen that with my father. He admits that he's a man of little imagination but he's had disheartening opinions about my efforts in fields where he has ***no*** experience.

On the other hand . . . imagine having dinner with *smart, supportive people who want you to succeed.*

Which people? Walt Disney, Steve Jobs, Oprah Winfrey, Albert Einstein, Martin Luther King, Jr., Helen Keller, and John Lasseter.

There is something that these seven people share: *They're great communicators.*

So this book will help you become a great communicator. The fun part is that we'll cover empowering ideas shared by these notable people. Then, I'll share material that will help you develop your own communication skills.

Our first topic for the dinner gathering is one's personal brand.

Walt Disney said, "You know I'm not Walt Disney anymore. Walt Disney is a thing. You know Walt Disney doesn't smoke. I smoke. Walt Disney doesn't drink. I drink."

I turned to Oprah* and said, "You have a terrific personal brand."

She replied, *"The struggle of my life created empathy—I could relate to pain, being abandoned, having people not love me."*

I suggested, "That's why people connect with you, Oprah."

So now we'll talk about communication. Sections like the following are similar to after dinner conversations. I've had opportunities to learn great ideas from people at dinner and then further explore those ideas when talking with a friend one on one.

****

* **NOTE:** Since 70% of the people in the imagined dinner gathering are dead . . . yes, the idea of these people at one table is fiction. ***However, each quote is from a credible source.***

Consider this book as my chance to coach you one on one after we've encountered some great dinner talk from the seven notable people.

Want to make more money? In business, you can create lots of good results. More sales. Getting a raise. Producing more profit. Winning promotions. Ending up with more money, more respect, more authority.

Sounds good. Now what? Consider communication. The exchange of information. Not just facts and figures, but opinions and insights. Understanding markets, employees and managers. The best communicators in business make the most money. They get offered more opportunities. Why? Because people trust them. How do you build that trust?—through a great ***personal brand***. Consider standard business brands. Mention Disney and people think "family entertainment." In fact, some researchers report that Disney owns the label "family entertainment." It simply is Disney's brand.

Consider Kleenex. How many times have you said, "Pass me the Kleenex?" Kleenex in essence owns the brand of "facial tissue." Some companies create great success built on a vivid, successful brand.

Now think of your personal brand. If someone were to say your name, what five words would come up in anyone's mind?

What's the fast track to business success? It's to build a great personal brand.

What is a personal brand? The fast answer relates to this question: *"What are you best known for?"* My clients have answered:

- I'm known for creative solutions under extreme pressure.
- I'm known as someone everyone can rely on.

- I'm known as always prepared, for thinking of how things might go wrong.

You build your personal brand by everything you say and what actions you take. Your personal brand communicates:
- Who I am
- What you can count on me to do
- What I expect from life

"What I expect from life" is a vital part of your personal brand because it's how you can attract opportunities and business. Your habitual ways of talking hopefully convey your *positive* expectations that you may not voice but *people subconsciously pick up the meaning.* Here are some positive, non-spoken expectations: "I expect to be successful. I will complete tough projects. People enjoy being around me. People find me to be trustworthy."

The truth is: you already have a personal brand. The important thing is to take conscious control of how you shape it and improve it.

Some personal brands help people move forward faster. Other personal brands create undue stress and career stalls.

Many people hear of a personal brand as something that helps for job interviews and marketing. In this book, we'll go beyond that. *Your personal brand becomes the mode for* ***all*** *business communication.*

While striving for success, people want to know business pitfalls and they want *countermeasures.* Each "Secret" that follows takes that as its premise. All communication in business makes a difference. Each piece of feedback, voicemail, announcement, managerial decision, reaction to a managerial decision, even organizing the office New Year's Party–it all matters, one way or another. All of them.

Without exception.

Through this book, I'll act as your coach. You'll learn countermeasures so you avoid traps, but better than that, you'll excel in your career. You'll discover literally hundreds of ways to build your positive personal brand.

Let's begin.

SECRET #1: YOU TRAIN PEOPLE HOW TO TREAT YOU.

Your time is limited, so don't waste it living someone else's life. Don't be trapped by dogma—which is living with the results of other people's thinking. Don't let the noise of others' opinions drown out your own inner voice. And most important, have the courage to follow your heart and intuition. — Steve Jobs

Have you noticed that people who follow their own path often radiate charisma? Steve Jobs radiated such intense charisma that numerous people said he created a "reality distortion field." That is, he could convince people that his vision was truer than the reality they thought they knew. Often, Steve Jobs was correct: his team *could* do something that appeared impossible to accomplish in the time constraints they faced.

In essence, Steve Jobs trained people to go along with his extraordinary plans.

Have you noticed that successful people get better treatment? They receive the better assignments, more promotions and bigger raises. What many rarely notice is the order in which this happens. Naturally enough, we assume that achieving all that equals success. The perks show that a person is in fact successful. Receiving them literally defines what success is. True enough. Up to a point. But also true is that people can do this the other way round, by creating the impression that they are already successful. In other words, they train people how to treat them. And this process remains deeply rooted in your personal brand.

Your personal brand is built on the stories you tell and by the actions you take.

Before we go further, a word about "stories." I've heard people say, "With my luck the traffic will make me late for dinner." That's a downer comment that implies a downer story of one unlucky event after another for a lifetime! Such a story is detrimental to anyone's personal brand. So when I say story, I mean more than an anecdote. I'm also talking about *these little self-detrimental comments* we say casually.

These stories and actions center on three elements of your personal brand, three details that define your personal brand, your identity and reputation in the workplace.

a) Who I am.

b) What you can count on me to do.

c) What I expect from life.

This last detail, "what I expect from life," is embodied in this example:

Sarah's personal brand is "the one upon whom everyone relies." She even reinforces this personal brand when she says, "That's when Cheryl (the supervisor) said, 'Sarah, I can always rely on you.'" Well and good. As far as that goes.

When some co-workers look on her as a patsy, then Sarah has a problem. *The American Heritage Dictionary* defines *patsy* as "a person easily taken advantage of, cheated, blamed, or ridiculed."

Case in point: George works with Sarah. He procrastinates, knowing full well that Sarah will stay late. Maybe she's trying to help him protect his job. Perhaps she simply refuses to allow everyone else to suffer from George's failures. She might focus so exclusively upon the task, she pays no real attention to how George takes advantage. Why, hardly matters, not in this context.

Pay close attention here: Sarah's behavior speaks loudly. Her actions say "I expect to overwork, to help others even when inappropriate. I expect others to take advantage."

Soon another co-worker Mira asks, "Sarah, did you stay late again and help George?"

With a rueful smile, Sarah sighs and says, "Well, you know how George is. I don't want him to get into trouble..."

Mira shakes her head. But guess what? Mira too will lean on Sarah when she needs help. After all, Sarah just gave her permission!

Sarah endured being socialized as a "nice girl." Author Lois P. Frankel invites women to take charge of their own lives and transform from a "nice girl" to a "Winning Woman." A nice girl placates; a winning woman stands up for herself. Women make the tough choices and reap the rewards. What tough choices? One choice is to dig deep and discover what is holding one back and to take action to improve one's situation.

Before we go further, men reading this book also know about the pressure to be a "nice guy." Sometimes, one has to take a stand and endure some flack.

The problem for Sarah is her personal brand is incomplete. Her solution would be to have ***a Personal Brand with "And."*** Things would go better with a personal brand of "reliable and fair." By this we mean, *fair to herself* and fair to others. It's not fair for Sarah to take on inappropriate work and to stay late to help procrastinating George.

With this example of "reliable and fair" you're getting an inkling of what a personal brand is. I began this book by referring to your personal brand as an answer to the question: "What are you best known for."

Let's explore a brief overview of some thoughts on personal branding:

• *"Your personal brand is a promise to your clients... a promise of quality, consistency, competency, and reliability." — Jason Hartman*

• *"A great brand taps into emotions. Emotions drive most, if not all, of our decisions. A brand reaches out with a powerful connecting experience. It's an emotional connecting point that transcends the product." — Scott Bedbury*

• *"Personal branding takes your skills, your personality, and your unique characteristics and packages them into a powerful identity that will lift you above the crowd of anonymous competitors. Personal branding is actually a very simple concept. It's who you are, what you do, and what makes you unique. Personal branding controls how other people perceive you." — Peter Montoya*

I'll add: *Personal branding is a way of being in the world and your total approach to communicating.*

Earlier, I shared that we all have a personal brand. This book is about taking conscious control of your personal brand and improving it to the benefit of your career and life.

Sarah has a negative personal brand: "reliable and over accommodating." Another way to view the situation: She thinks her personal brand is "Captain Reliable." But in truth she comes across as "Little Miss Walk All Over Me."

What Sarah needs is an ***Empowered Personal Brand***—which shows one as competent, pleasant and effective. Here are examples of phrases my client Mark says to showcase his personal brand:

a) *Who I am:* "I'm feeling good. I anticipated that ____ would happen and I took good care of the client." [Who is Mark? Someone who is aware, proactive and generally positive.]

b) *What you can count on me to do:* "Just as I promised, here is the report. On schedule, in the correct format, with an extra copy just in case."

c) *What I expect from life:* "Wow! I feel so lucky. Jonah Cliante referred me to the top person at 1-2-3, Inc. It's looking good that I'll be bringing in their business." [Mark feels lucky. He expects good things to happen. He expects to do the right things to bring in more business.]

Recently, I asked my public speaking course college students: "Do you want to stand next to an unlucky person?" They laughed in response, likely picturing lightning striking both the unlucky person and the hapless person standing nearby.

As you can see from Mark's above comments, a personal brand, in essence, is *an on-going story* you are telling the world. Make sure that the details that issue from *your mouth* emphasize your competence, good demeanor and trustworthiness.

One of my favorite stories about someone seizing a pivotal moment and upgrading their personal brand comes from author and corporate consultant Kathleen Reardon. When she was a young researcher, she had the opportunity to join luminaries in her field on a panel, addressing the audience at a professional conference. A bombastic professor stood up and denigrated her and her work, stating she was too young to have brought anything of value to the panel.

Feelings churned in Ms. Reardon's body. She had written a well-regarded book, but she was young and relatively new to the field. Then, from the audience, her friend caught her eye and mimed a fist slamming into her other hand—in the manner of "Crush him."

Finally, the bombastic professor sat down after a terrible 20 minutes. And Reardon stood up. Making her voice as calm as possible, she said:

"I could spend my whole twenty minutes with you today responding to my colleague, but that would be a decided waste of our time. Let me start my presentation by quoting him, an indication that at least I've actually *read* his work."

The audience roared with laughter. Soon they applauded.

Now, I ask you. What was Kathleen Reardon's personal brand at that point?

Imagine you're in that audience. What are you thinking? I'm thinking: *here is an effective professional who is confident in her own skills and her own work. I'm interested in listening to what she has to say.*

Let's look deeper. Reardon comes across as *confident but coachable.* How? She has read her opponent's work. She demonstrates that she keeps up with the insights of others in her field. That's coachable.

Confident but coachable is an example of what I call a *Power Combo of a Personal Brand.* Using such a combo truly improves your personal brand. How? It provides you with a positive attribute plus a balancing additional characteristic.

Let's return to Sarah's problem: Her negative personal brand is "reliable and over accommodating." An improvement would be a Power Combo "reliable but fair" or something like "friendly but efficient."

To make that her improved personal brand, Sarah must expand her "tool kit" of behaviors. When Mira, attempting to follow in George's footsteps, tries to get Sarah to help her, Sarah says, "Mira, that sounds tough to deal with. And . . . let's check with Cheryl (their supervisor) and get her input." We can see that Sarah is *not* going to keep Mira's secret of not being able to do her own work. It's true that situations like this require diplomacy and tact. But the point is that Sarah is not going to deplete her own resources in ways that may make her miss her own deadlines, required by Cheryl.

It's important that Sarah think through and rehearse ways of responding before she is next confronted with an inappropriate request. Sarah could say:

a) Mira, I hear you. And as you know, I'd need a formal written request.

b) Mira, I can relate to that. And my plate is full. You might ask Cheryl about what you can do.

To develop effective ways to respond, **do some self-reflection and deliberately choose what elements you want for your personal brand.**

Here are other Power Combo examples:

- Tough but fair
- Someone who values her own time and respects yours.

Three Methods to Improve Your Personal Brand

1) Agree with the Feeling—but Do Not Solve The Other Person's Problem.

We notice that Sarah said, "Mira, that sounds tough to deal with." That creates space for Mira's feelings. Sarah acknowledged how Mira felt in the moment. This is a diplomatic way to connect with a co-worker.

Let's look at the opposite tack. What if Sarah said abruptly: "Yeah. Well, I gotta get back to work." That may be true, but Sarah may needlessly turn Mira into an enemy.

For her next step, Sarah said, "And . . . let's check with Cheryl and get her input." Sarah does *not* solve Mira's problem. Now, Cheryl, as their supervisor, will need to do *her* job and lead them both.

2) Avoid Devaluing Yourself

Trudy, one of my clients, would often say to friends " . . . well, you know. I'm weird." Her friends would tease Trudy about saving money to hire a screenplay consultant and devoting most of her free time to writing a screenplay. I advised Trudy to replace the "I'm weird" remark with taking a breath. Trudy was not weird—instead "she was thoroughly *herself*." Her friends may tease her, but the truth is: they do *not* want what Trudy wants and they're not willing to pay the price. Trudy needs to walk her own path.

3) Avoid Saying "I'm Sorry" when Inappropriate

Have you noticed this? Some people say, "I'm sorry" too

much. They need an expanded vocabulary. If something disappointing happens to a friend, you can say with sincerity: "I'm sad to hear about the tough situation you're enduring." Saying "I'm sorry" too much, for some people is a defense mechanism that basically comes across as "Look, I'm small and harmless. Don't hurt me."

You can express compassion without devaluing yourself. Saying "I'm sorry" too much creates the impression that you're weak. Who would you give a vital project to—someone who is weak or someone who is strong and competent?

Some people may say that taking on blame is the problem, not two simple words "I'm sorry." I see that point, and I'm adding that saying "I'm sorry" too much *creates the impression* that you are doing wrong. It makes it look like it's your fault. That does *not* help your personal brand.

As noted earlier, your personal brand is a promise of quality, consistency, competency, and reliability.

Our first Secret is: You train people how to treat you. And how is that done? By the little things you casually say. So stop that! Become conscious about how everything you say can either improve your personal brand or destroy it.

As we wind down to close this particular topic, let's notice other negative ways people train others in how to treat them:

- If one routinely lies to people, the person trains others to lie to them.
- If one pushes limits to see what he can get away with, he encourages the same in others.
- If one engages in personal dramas in the workplace, the person trains people to respond to her on that level.
- If one distrusts everyone, the person trains others to distrust them.

Let's turn this around. Make your positive personal brand emphasize: honesty, creativity and focus. This makes for a better personal brand.

- **Secret #1: You train people how to treat you.**

- **Your Countermeasure:**

Make deliberate choices as to what you want your personal brand to mean to other people. Choose a *Power Combo* like: "friendly and efficient" or "tough but fair" or some other combination that means a lot to you. Avoid devaluing yourself. Demonstrate: who you are, what people can count on you to do and what (positive things) you expect in life.

SECRET #2: GOING TOO FAST WASTES TIME.

Disneyland will never be completed. It will continue to grow as long as there is imagination left in the world. - Walt Disney

Walt Disney was famous for taking the required time to complete something with quality. For example, right in the middle of making the feature film, *Pinocchio,* he shut down production. Why? He said simply that the production had no heart. He did not restart production until he and his team, added Jiminy Cricket, the cute, warm, sweet-singing character who served as Pinocchio's conscience. Walt honored that quality demanded more effort and more time.

To do things with quality, often you must devote the *required time* so that you accomplish something correctly *the first time.*

In our dinner gathering, Albert Einstein emphasized, *"Make everything as simple as possible, but not simpler."*

I have a quick thought about how people try a so-called "simple solution" of using email to quickly solve something.

This ever happen to you? Something comes up. You decide to handle it simply and quickly. The solution? Email! An email message goes out, using as few words as possible to make the point. Within twenty minutes, an hour at most, responses to your email start flooding the mailbox. People want clarification. Some think you're blaming them. Others just don't understand what you're saying. A couple may be angry at your tone, for the way they think you insulted them (and maybe their departments), the manner with which you worded things. One simple, fast email just became a *situation* to be managed, and if managed wrong can cause problems for weeks, maybe months.

First, I empathize that you have too much to do. During the current economic recession, many businesses lay off employees and merely drop the extra work on the few remaining employees. And those of us who own businesses often find that we're "wearing too many hats."

Because everyone else is also busy, they may overreact to your simple email, but in their minds they haven't. Are they right? Wrong? Here's something to consider, something you might even find freeing: It doesn't matter. What does matter? *Results.* On a moment by moment basis, you cannot control how people read or listen. So develop the habit of taking an extra few moments (or seconds) to interact carefully. Among other things, this encourages others to do the same thing with listening and reading.

Save yourself time and grief by approaching each interaction with care. You do *not* have to take a lot of time. Pause for a moment. Just a moment. **To avoid going too fast, ask yourself three questions:**

1) How are people feeling now?

2) Does this person feel heard?

3) How can I repeat what I heard and confirm I

understood what they meant?

One way to remember these questions is *"Feelings–Heard–Repeat."*

Taking an extra moment now can prevent a misunderstanding. With everyone moving fast and feeling on edge, misunderstandings are more likely. Small things lead to big messes. A number of people more easily take offense. Now, we'll explore each question:

1) How are people feeling now?

Emotions matter. Don't believe anyone who says otherwise. Feelings can inspire, motivate, energize and increase efficiency. They can also distract, confuse and turn an office into a hive of petty insults and battlegrounds. Research bears this out: Pay people for what they were doing for fun and many will stop enjoying themselves. Then they stop doing it! Even though they're being paid! Quite possibly *because* they're being paid. It became a chore. A burden. A duty. So we have empirical evidence that feelings cause behavior changes. It's helpful to take into account what the other person may feel in response to what you do.

When writing an email, I imagine how the person will *feel* reading my words. Often, I go back and change the beginning of my message. Why? Because I want to help the person feel good and receptive to the rest of my message. I often thank someone for their good work. And, if appropriate, I mention the context of what the vision is and what outcomes we're working toward.

By the way, I try to address the person by name during emails. Many of us dread email. Just one more request/order/instruction—as if we don't have enough already. Hence the using of names, the thanking for previous efforts and the like. Anything reasonable to make co-workers feel better makes them work better.

At this point, you may think that the above advice only relates to emails. Actually, adding warm elements to your phone conversations and in-person discussions does much to smooth the way for more efficiency—and a pleasant work environment.

Think of it this way: with each co-worker you have an "emotional bank account." When you address the person warmly, you deposit into that bank account. When you request some action on their part, you're making a withdrawal. In this context, you probably see how it's so important to put positive deposits into this emotional bank account.

Feelings matter so much that you may drain the emotional bank account inadvertently. In this section we're asking the question: *How are people feeling now?* Ask yourself: How am I feeling now?

Why is that important? You can inadvertently exude a bad mood that has nothing to do with the other person, but it still can cause difficulties.

For example, sometimes I work at home. A family member comes into the room with her own problem. I'll listen as well as I can. When appropriate, I'll add: "You're important to me. I hope you understand that I may be distracted. I have 78 more papers to grade for college students. So I'm feeling on edge at the moment."

One family member said, "I'm glad you told me that. I thought you were upset with me."

At work, you need to use tact and discretion. It would not help to appear to be overly sensitive. But it can be wise to say something like: "I'm distracted by needing to finish this report for Susan. How about I stop by your office at 3 pm to talk about this?"

When you're at work, you'll want to plan how you would talk about being preoccupied. It's not helpful to say, "I'm in a bad mood." Instead, when you say, "I'm distracted by needing to finish this report for Susan," that's a legitimate business-related situation.

2) Does this person feel heard?

One extremely common feeling in any workplace remains frustration. All too often it feels as if one's words go ignored. We've all experienced this. None of us like it. And very nearly all of us have inspired such feelings in others—rarely on purpose. If people feel unheard, ignored, invisible they quite naturally feel frustrated.

Where does all that frustration go? Nowhere. That's the problem: It stays put and festers. Like a disease. Or a time bomb. We have to do something to defuse the bomb. I often end phone conversations with: "Is there anything else you need me to know?" This gives the person the chance to think for a moment and see if there is something else she wants to say to me. Often, the person adds some details. Then, I'll summarize our conversation and check-in with the person so that I know she feels I've heard and understood her message.

In this section we're talking about *Secret #2: Going too fast wastes time.* Asking yourself the question, Does this person feel heard? helps you *pause and slow down*. Make space for the person's feelings. You can ask another question like: "Are you okay with this?" This opens the door for the other person to access how they're feeling. Another version is: "Do you feel okay with this?"

So much business conversation focuses on the rational mind with questions like: "What do you think, Stephanie?"

However, a lot of the energy to get things done originates in feelings. So make sure that you ask questions so that the person feels heard—not just for what she thinks but also for what she feels.

Some readers may feel that this is too touchy-feely for work. In my discussions with top successful people, I've learned what true leadership entails. Leaders gain loyalty. And loyalty is related to people's feelings. So it's wise to ensure that co-workers, clients and even one's supervisor feel that you care about their concerns.

3) How can I repeat what I heard and confirm I understood what they meant?

How do you know that the other person feels heard? Imagine you could assure them that you understood their meaning.

The method is to say something like, "I heard you say that ____ is important to you and you'd like me to double check with Nadia about this. Is that about right?"

At first glance these few words seem simple enough. On closer inspection, you'll notice that the words are well-chosen:

a) *"I heard you say—"* [You're not telling the person what they meant. You're expressing what you heard. This leaves room for the person to correct you and to give you more information.]

b) *"___ is important to you"* [You're identifying what you understand is personally important to the person. You're making a distinction. You're not saying what "is important to the company" for example. You need a light tone because some people may take offense if they think you're emphasizing *"to you* (and not important to others)." The solution is to say "to you" with the same tone as the rest of the sentence.]

c) *"Is that about right?"* [When you say "about," you're leaving space so the person can correct you and/or offer you more information. And that helps him or her feel heard.]

Be sure to use the person's words (as much as possible) and avoid straying too far away with paraphrasing their message.

Some readers may be concerned about "sounding like a parrot" if one only repeats exactly what the speaker said. Here's an example:

- Robert: "We've got to finish Report 1-7 by Friday. I don't want to be on the hook for the client's getting upset."
- Susan: "I heard you say that you don't want to be on the hook — so we must complete Report 1-7 by Friday?"

Susan did not repeat Robert's words exactly but she did use his language of "don't want to be on the hook."

You do not always need to use "Is that about right?" But if someone does provide further clarification, repeat your new understanding of what you heard to the speaker's satisfaction. In this way, the speaker finally feels heard and understood.

Now, how does this relate to your personal brand? It helps if you get the personal brand of someone who makes other people feel important.

Everyone has an invisible sign hanging from their neck saying, 'Make me feel important.' Never forget this message when working with people. — Mary Kay Ash

When you take a few moments to make sure the person feels heard and that her feelings are respected, you save a lot of time.

As we wind down this particular topic, it's valuable to look at another source of misunderstandings. I have focused on feelings, and now we'll look at data. A subtle but pervasive problem in communication remains how we use identical words and phrases to mean subtly different things. "The deadline is Friday" seems so straightforward, but does it mean:

1. Turn it in first thing Friday morning.
2. You have until end of business on Friday.
3. It goes out into the post on Friday.
4. Friday is too late, we need it by Thursday.

The above indicates all kinds of possible misunderstandings. That's why I called this section: *Secret #2: Going too fast wastes time.*

Imagine how much disruption of efficiency and how much emotional turmoil can occur if two people hold different ideas of "The deadline is Friday."

Remember the trio of questions:

1) How are people feeling now?

2) Does this person feel heard?

3) How can I repeat what I heard and confirm I understood what they meant?

As we discussed, one way to remember these questions is *"Feelings–Heard–Repeat."*

In particular, when you get to the third question, you can say things like:

- I want to make sure we're on the same page. Does "the deadline is Friday" mean you need the report at 9 AM

Friday morning?"

- Friday? I want to make sure things go well. You need it for the 2 pm meeting with Nadia—do I have that right?

From the above, you can see how a few gentle questions to clarify people's meanings can be truly helpful.

The single biggest problem in communication is the illusion that it has taken place. — George Bernard Shaw

This process all boils down to taking just a few moments to clarify some details. You'll save so much time and avoid so much emotional turmoil, that it's really worth rehearsing how you address your business conversations.

- **Secret #2: Going too fast wastes time.**

- **Your Countermeasure:**

Remember *Feelings—Heard—Repeat.* Add a few moments to ensure that the other person feels heard. Ask gentle clarifying questions so that you avoid causing a mess that needlessly swallows your time.

SECRET #3: PEOPLE LOVE TO BUY, BUT HATE BEING SOLD.

A lot of times, people don't know what they want until you show it to them. - Steve Jobs

In our dinner gathering, Steve Jobs comment stirred a little controversy.

Walt Disney agreed with Steve Jobs and said, *"[In my company,] we keep moving forward, opening new doors, and doing new things, because we're curious and curiosity keeps leading us down new paths."*

I agreed with both of them. And still I added something to the mix. Ever see a customer nearly jump to the ceiling when a salesman comes up out of nowhere and asks, "May I help you?"

"I'm just browsing!" the customer exclaims defensively.

What did the salesman do wrong? He asked a question that elicits a reflexive negative response from the customer. On the other hand, I trained (years ago) in how to sell jewelry. I learned it's better to ask, "So what brings you into the store today?"

How does this work better? First, you avoid the annoying "May I help you?" question. You also *avoid* the customer's brain jumping to thoughts that you're intruding and pressing for a sale. Second, you're inviting a person to explore his or her reasons for exploring the store. The customer focuses on the *feelings he or she wants to gain from buying a product.*

And here's my point. When I said to our dinner guests, "You're inviting a person to explore his or her reasons for exploring the store," I suggested that it's important to support a customer in feeling autonomous. That detail, in a way, conflicts with Steve Jobs approach of, in essence, he knows what the customers will want.

This section will help you invite and gain cooperation from anyone with whom you interact: clients, co-workers, a supervisor . . . even teenagers.

This section is about *"People love to buy, but hate being sold."* By the way, "buy" can also refer to "buy an idea or agree to cooperate."

In our dinner gathering, Martin Luther King, Jr. talked about leading people to better things. He said, *"Darkness cannot drive out darkness; only light can do that. Hate cannot drive out hate; only love can do that."*

In essence, Martin Luther King, Jr. talked about showing people a vision.

So that brings us back to Steve Jobs. It is certain that he always promoted a vision. He said, "I want to put a ding in the universe." By context, we understood that he wanted to lead his team to change the world.

I agreed with the idea of holding a vision and I added that when a person buys into an idea they feel strong. They are empowered to take positive action (just like Steve Jobs' team did when following his lead).

Let's look at the differences between "buy" and "sold":

To buy is . . .

- to feel powerful (I want that—now I got it!)
- to make a good decision and bring benefits into one's life

To be sold is . . .

- to be pushed and manipulated.
- to feel weak.
- to lose one's autonomy.

To feel autonomous consists of experiencing one's power of having unfettered choices. On the other hand, novice salespeople may come on too strong. By pushing, the novice salesperson threatens the potential buyer's autonomy. And that relates to people's subconscious negative reaction to "May I help you?" It does not come across as a genuine and caring question. It feels so perfunctory. And it's part of a novice salesperson invading one's personal space. That's why the other question: "So what brings you into the store today?" is helpful. The question immediately focuses on the customer's feelings and priorities.

Some may say: "I don't need to sell anything." Actually, successful people sell their ideas all of the time. Successful people get cooperation. How do they do that? Successful people I've interviewed have described their methods to me.

And now, I have distilled the ideas into a three-point process:

- Don't sell—attract.
- Don't push—invite.
- Don't talk a lot—listen

1) Don't sell—attract.

Instead of telling someone what's good about a product, a pro-salesperson asks gentle questions to bring up a buyer's reasons for a purchase. In essence, the pro-salesperson helps the buyer tune in to her own desires and reasons. I use the term "pro-salesperson" because we've all met novice salespeople who really don't seem to know how to serve a customer. Many of us would like to say, "I don't think this sales thing is working for you."

On the other hand, a pro-salesperson studies material like what you're reading here. They rehearse new methods and develop mastery of the art and science of selling.

Here's an example of a dialogue between a pro-salesperson and a customer:

Pro-salesperson: So what brings you into the store today?

Joseph: We're looking for some decorations for our living room mantle.

Pro-salesperson: Oh, that's an important part of the home. So did you have any thoughts in mind, some feelings about . . .?

Marina: Maybe some stylish picture frames for our most important photos.

Pro-salesperson: Sounds great. What *are* your favorite photos? What feeling would you like to have when you gaze upon them?

As you can see from the above dialogue, the pro-salesperson guides the person toward both thoughts and feelings.

How is this process about attraction? A customer is *not* attracted to the salesperson's reasons for the purchase. Naturally, the customer is attracted to her *own* personal desires and reasons. Some salespeople have said, "You're really selling to the person part of herself. Her own feelings. Her own priorities. And her own desire to overcome fears and find solutions."

Here is an oft-told principle: *People buy on emotion and later justify on facts.* This means that a salesperson or anyone seeking to gain cooperation needs to speak in the "language of emotion." Get someone to have what researchers call a "wanting." That is, the person wants some outcome and you help them see that they can satisfy their desire. Then, give the person some logical reasons to justify their emotional choice. They'll want the logical reasons to express to someone they'll need to justify their choice to (a spouse, a sibling, a co-worker or supervisor).

Remember: Help a person connect with his or her own feelings.

2) Don't push—invite.

People buy for *their* reasons, *not* yours. In many cases, simple logical reasons to make a purchase are not enough to get someone to actually buy the product or service.

Invite the person to explore their personal reasons. Again, it's about gentle questions. A gentle question sounds like: "So what good result would you enjoy when you own this product?"

On the other hand a "harsh question" would sound like: "What problem would occur if you don't buy this product today?"

Some novice salespersons take one step forward and two

steps back. They try to "educate" the buyer. On the one hand this means they come across as an expert. But they also seem arrogant, insufferable and pushy. Remember, few people like to feel herded. Helped, yes. Waited upon, definitely. Advised, certainly. But treated like a very young, extremely ignorant child? No way. Many of them become angry.

Instead of assuming the role of Authority Figure, become the trusted advisor. How? Use your light tone and supportive comments to invite the buyer to take advantage of your expertise as they see fit.

Here's an example:

Pro-salesperson: This new room sounds like a great addition to your home. So where would you like to start? Paneling, drapes, shelving? I can help mix and match if you'd like. When you're in this room, how do you want to feel?

Sarah: I've always wanted a room that feels a bit rustic. The wood paneling is important to me. I want to sit down, look around and feel like I'm in another world. A slower time."

From this sample dialogue, you can see that the pro-salesperson assists the buyer to explore what she wants.

3) Don't talk a lot—listen.

Above, the process of *invite* included asking questions to help the buyer to explore what she wants and even to *listen* to herself.

After the buyer has explored her own desires and reasons, she will naturally ask you questions. When you respond to the buyer's questions, keep your answers, if possible, down to 20 seconds (or less). Why? You want to return the "conversation spotlight" back to the buyer as fast as possible. Ask another question to help the buyer drill down to more feelings and reasons.

Asking questions is a foundation to helping someone buy a product or agree to your suggestion. Now, we'll go even deeper into the process. What you need to do is: *Discover someone's buying strategy*. And this process is something I've taught clients and graduate students for more than a decade.

For someone to come to a decision they actually progress through three stages: *input, processing* and *closure.* Hence their buying strategy consists of their individual preferences as embodied in these stages of *input, processing* and *closure.*

Let's break this down.

Input: At the beginning of an interaction, the buyer will take in information (input). She has a natural preference for one of three modalities: visual, auditory or kinesthetic (related to body senses and touch). Some buyers (like me) prefer to see something like a website (a visual preference). Others like to get information by hearing you talk about details; that would be someone who prefers the auditory modality. You might notice a buyer paying close attention to how something feels—like the fabric of a chair (a kinesthetic preference).

Processing: After receiving input, the buyer now needs to put things together in their own thinking and feelings. Some people (like me) prefer a kinesthetic approach; I prefer to use a calculator and *prove to myself* what cost savings may occur if I purchase some product. Again, when we look at any phase of the three (input, processing and closure), we notice that a buyer will have a preference related to the modalities (visual, auditory and kinesthetic).

Closure: After input and processing, the buyer needs to firm up in her own mind what her decision will be. Purchase, postpone or reject the product? Again a preference related to visual, auditory or kinesthetic is involved. Some buyers (like me) prefer to *hear* testimonials; I prefer to talk with previous buyers and hear their testimonial in real time. I'll ask questions and see how any rough patch was handled by the salesperson and her company.

So now, I'll summarize my own buying strategy.

Input: Visual. (I see the website, view a quick video, read a testimonial.)

Processing: Kinesthetic. (I prove any cost savings to myself; I double-check the numbers with a calculator.)

Closure: Auditory. (I talk with previous customers and hear about their experiences.)

As you saw above, the three modalities of visual, auditory and kinesthetic can apply to each phase of buying.

The question that comes up is: *How do you know what modality per phase (input, processing or closure) is what the buyer prefers?*

The answer to the question is an involved process I call: *Deep Listening and Giving Key Responses.* A response may be a particular question or a particular answer—it depends on what you observe the buyer do. It varies by the moment.

So we begin with Deep Listening. You listen carefully to the buyer's words.

Visual: I ***see*** your point. . . It looked good to me.

Auditory: I ***hear*** you . . . I heard all I needed to know.

Kinesthetic: It just didn't ***feel*** right to me. . . . Oh, yes. The meeting went ***smoothly***. . . . No, I don't think Mark will be a ***good fit*** with the team.

The above examples come from the science of neurolinguistic programming. Over several years, a number of studies and people's action results have verified the value of observing the modalities (visual, auditory and kinesthetic) and then making an appropriate response.

So how do you discover what people want as input? You ask a question like:

"In order for you to feel you know this product, what has to happen?" To ask the above question takes practice. Also, consider modifying the question so that it feels comfortable coming from your mouth.

Then, listen for clues:

- "I'll need to ***see*** some graphs about the results." (Visual)
- "I'd like to ***hear*** what your previous customers feel about the product. Is there someone I can talk with?" (Auditory)
- "I'd need to ***'test drive'*** this product. How about you guide me as I try it." (Kinesthetic)

In the classroom, sometimes my graduate students ask for further clarification about *kinesthetic people.* I give myself as an example: If a team member is going to show me how to use a function in a particular software program, I need to be in the chair and clicking the mouse. It doesn't work if they "just show it to me."

Now, we'll talk about *processing* (phase two of a person's buying strategy). How do you discover what the buyer's processing preference is? Ask a question like: "So how do you like to go through these details to see if this product is a match for you?" The operative words here are *like to go through these details.*

The third phase of someone's buying strategy is *closure.* Sometime during a conversation—if you can—you ask about the buyer's process when she made a previous purchase.

You might ask something like: *So how did it go? When did you know that the car was the right one for you?* [We'll use purchasing a car as an example here.]

The person may reply:

- I felt the power of the engine. (Kinesthetic)
- I caught a glimpse of the car and me driving—reflected off the showroom window. (Visual)
- Well . . . my wife said, "This car is you, Joe." (Auditory). [You need to watch the buyer carefully. In this example, we notice that Joe *listened* to his wife's affirmation of the buying decision.]

Helping people buy is really about being a facilitator. *The Merriam-Webster Dictionary* defines *facilitator* as "one that helps to bring about an outcome (as learning, productivity, or communication) by providing indirect or unobtrusive assistance, guidance, or supervision." These are the noteworthy words, *indirect or unobtrusive assistance.* Facilitating is subtle.

On the other hand, too many of us fall into the trap of trying to educate the buyer. We probably do that because of conditioning related to lectures by parents and early teachers. They were trying to *teach us* something.

Instead, as a facilitator, you *help the person discover for herself* what she feels and what her priorities are.

Sure, you're the expert. But you aim to be the *trusted advisor,* helping with details that the buyer *wants* to hear more about.

To increase your opportunities to gain cooperation, think deeply about the other person's feelings and priorities. Devote lots of energy to listening. By the way, people with an effective personal brand are known for: a) being interested in other people and b) being a good listener.

You start listening faster because you practice good questions. How is this important? Researchers note that people tend to be self-centered. They're busy feeling various pressures and even the fear of making mistakes. When you listen, you demonstrate that you care about the person. You're there to help the person get her needs met.

When you're listening, you're winning.

• Secret #3: People love to buy, but hate being sold.

• Your Countermeasure:

Rehearse until you become comfortable with asking gentle questions. Practice listening. Restrain yourself from telling or pushing people about what you think should happen. Instead, guide the person to experience how to fulfill their own feelings and needs. Remember to attract, invite and listen to the other person.

SECRET #4: HOLDING A FACADE OF "BEING PERFECT" CAN PARALYZE YOU AND TORPEDO A TEAM'S LOYALTY.

Every single Pixar film, at one time or another, has been the worst movie ever put on film. But we know. We trust our process. We don't get scared and say, "Oh, no, this film isn't working"
- John Lasseter

John Lasseter has led Pixar's filmmaking efforts for several years. He is currently the chief creative officer of both Pixar and Walt Disney Studios. During our dinner gathering, when he said, "We trust our process," he talked about how Pixar films go through many stages. All along the way, team members are empowered to express their concerns about any element that seems to be going wrong.

One of my relatives cannot admit to being wrong. And I do *not* trust him. I do not trust that he will step away from his personal disdain for people. I cannot trust he will improve in how he works with others. *When a person cannot admit error, he cannot improve.* Why? Because he will not allow new ideas or coaching to influence him. Tragic really. Nor am I alone. People realize this person cannot be trusted to face harsh realities, his personal weaknesses—and to protect the group's best interests.

Some people become masters of the "cover up"—well, they *think* they are until they're caught. Several politicians have been caught in scandals. They tried to appear to be "the perfect candidate." That didn't work. Holding a facade of "being perfect" causes several problems:

- You'll lose time and energy covering up mistakes.
- People will see through your cover-up efforts and henceforth distrust you.
- You'll get paralyzed and avoid appropriate risks because you'll be playing not to lose instead of playing to win.
- You miss the opportunity to gain real loyalty from team members.

Let's explore elements of the above problems:

• ***You'll lose time and energy covering up mistakes.***

Years ago, I worked as part of the technology group that insured that a particular bank had the first online banking system. One of the department leaders spoke of "fail forward fast." The goal was to be the first bank to accomplish online banking. The deadlines were fierce. And that meant that we needed to uncover faults in the prototype banking system fast. No cover-ups. No hiding. There were no perfect programmers. They made errors and bugs in the code popped up. And the team eliminated them as fast as possible. This was a highly functional team that met the deadline.

• ***People will see through your cover-up efforts and henceforth distrust you.***

A twenty-year reputation can be lost in five minutes. If people catch you in a lie, then from that moment on, they'll have doubts about your trustworthiness. Avoid lying. You might say something like: "What I can tell you is ____" and say only what you deem appropriate. The powerful approach would be to say, "I made an error. And here is my plan to avoid such a mistake from this point forward." And also tell of how you're making up for any damage caused by the mistake. When you take responsibility, you are trustworthy.

• ***You'll get paralyzed and avoid appropriate risks because you'll be playing not to lose instead of playing to win.***

It's important to develop what's called "ego-strength." A strong person can admit an error and face consequences. A weak person will start by focusing on "not looking bad." That can be associated with "playing not to lose." To lose would look bad. Instead, a powerful personal brand would be: "Someone who assesses situations well and takes appropriate risks."

You miss 100 percent of the shots you don't take.
— Wayne Gretzky

Further, you would do well to be known as one who faces what could go wrong and who does not "bet the store." You take a risk but you're ready to minimize damage if something goes wrong. Again, this is a stronger position.

• ***You miss the opportunity to gain real loyalty from team members.***

"Deal in realities. Deal in truth," said Jim Rohn, a top business leadership author and accomplished business owner. It's easier for people to give their loyalty to someone who *acknowledges mistakes, gets feedback and improves personal performance.* Such a leader demonstrates personal strength to face harsh realities—and to respond to coaching. And people like it when the leader listens to their counsel.

Good leaders admit their mistakes and fix the situation. Excellent professionals develop teams in which people pool their talents and the project becomes much more than what one person can do. Good leaders improve projects by fostering collaboration. Bad leaders spend too much time trying to appear "perfect" and covering their own mistakes. It does not work in the long run. For example, Mike Krzyzewski, Duke University basketball coach and author wrote: "When a leader makes a mistake and doesn't admit it, he is seen as arrogant and untrustworthy. And 'untrustworthy' is the last thing a leader wants to be."

Good leaders also shore up their personal weaknesses. Researchers note that many top professionals have talents or skills that act like two-edged swords. The hard-hitting leader often needs the "people person" second in command to take care of bumpy relations with team members. According to Disney insiders, CEO Michael Eisner and President and COO Frank Wells formed such a team. Frank Wells would smooth things over. Michael Eisner wrote: "It's inevitable in any work environment, and certainly all the more so in Hollywood: there are always going to be people working for you upset about something. At Disney, they went to Frank, and he would take them to lunch and find a solution to the problem." Many Disney employees felt a special loyalty to Frank Wells. Why? People feel loyal to those leaders who will hear them out.

For example, I have contractors who have worked on nine projects in a row with me. I ask for feedback, and often do *not* voice any opinion until I hear *their* words. Why? Because I seek to avoid a contractor trying to be nice and to self-censor her comment if she senses I have an opposite viewpoint. I want to hear multiple viewpoints; that gives me more options to improve the project. This process fosters a highly creative environment.

I thought a while about the next two quotes, and I realized that I wanted to share something I personally know and practice. For example, in describing my film directing style, actor and author David MacDowell Blue said, "Tom Marcoux treats cast and crew with great respect. He listens to ideas, allows a lot of give and take. Many directors remain defensive, even touchy about their own ideas. Tom always seems more interested in seeing what others can bring to a project. His support helped me express the truth in my scenes."

Actor/Director/Playwright/Producer Dan Wilson wrote: "As a director, Tom Marcoux consistently creates an environment where artists are encouraged to explore and discover the material, without compromising his own vision of the project. By allowing everyone to bring their best ideas to the table, Tom creates an environment that allows good work to thrive."

I include the above comments as examples of how professionals respond to leadership that focuses on collaboration. My team members feel free to alert me to details that are not working so I'll take action to get things fixed. I do not pretend to see everything. That's why I have an associate art director when I function as both writer and art director for graphic novels published by my company. She zeroes in on details I may have missed and I welcome her guidance. And she knows it. This makes for a successful working relationship.

In summary, let's remember to own up to mistakes and discard tendencies to try to appear "perfect."

• Secret #4: Holding a facade of "being perfect" can paralyze you and torpedo a team's loyalty.

• Your Countermeasure:

Open your awareness to when you're feeling uncomfortable. Ask yourself: Could my discomfort be visible on my face and in my body language (or vocal tone)? Assess if the situation would be helped by your telling the truth and owning up to some personal mistake. Pretending to be "perfect" only causes resentment and distrust. Be known (your personal brand) as someone who is aware of personal failings and who is working to improve personal performance.

SECRET #5: NO EXCUSES! LEARN TO LISTEN!

I am only one, but still I am one. I cannot do everything, but still I can do something; and because I cannot do everything, I will not refuse to do something that I can do. - Helen Keller

During our dinner conversation, when Helen Keller addressed us, we paid close attention. She was both blind and deaf so her constant companion Mrs. Anne Sullivan Macy sat with her to assist Helen's participation. In many ways, both Helen and her dear friend and teacher Anne embodied the patience and value of paying attention and listening to others. When Helen said, "I am only one, but still I am one. . . . I will not refuse to do something that I can do," it really shook us to the core.

What is one vital thing each of us can do? Listen well.

How do many people lose sales, promotions and raises? *They fail to listen well.*

This may be the most important section of this book—to assist you to rise to greater heights of success and fulfillment.

My father, now in his 70's, never learned to listen. It has cost him big time with work and family. But watching him inspired me to *avoid his habits*—to study and train in communication. *And listening is the major skill!*

Time and again, listening helped me take tough situations and make them better. I avoided a lot of needless conflict and wasted time because I listened instead of just talking.

When you listen well, a person feels heard. Until someone feels heard, tension builds. It often works best if you invite the other person to talk first. Then, they become more receptive to hear you.

Many people I've met truly do not know how to listen. What's the problem? It's like we're conditioned to do the wrong thing. People automatically engage in what I call *Three Listening Blockers:* judging, defending and "me, too — one up."

Let's explore the *Three Listening Blockers:*

a) Judging

We judge things automatically. Something doesn't fit right and we want to correct the other person immediately. Or our mouths stay shut, but our face and body language express disagreement or even disdain. Years ago, I visited a married couple at the hospital. Both worried for their newborn child who remained in intensive care for weeks. As we took a break for coffee, I noticed the wife constantly corrected her husband. He said, "We met some friends at 7 pm one night and—" And she said, "No, it was 6:30 pm, and—" In essence, she constantly judged every thing he said and found it lacking. She corrected him until he simply stopped talking.

Frankly, I was appalled. They were both hurting terribly

due to watching their child desperately cling to life. But her automatic judging denied him any comfort.

Instead of letting judgment gum up communication, I invite you to observe your automatic reaction to judge and try a method: the *Instant Reframe.*

The *Instant Reframe* is a new habit. Instead of judging, give the other person the benefit of the doubt. I once saw a bumper sticker that read: *Don't believe everything you think.* When you do an Instant Reframe, you take a first automatic negative thought and put it aside. You make sure that you can enter that next moment with, at least, a neutral approach.

Here's an example:

Susan: Women live longer than men.

Jack: [he thinks to himself: "Yeah. She's going to complain about how men are misguided again. Wait—I'm supposed to do an *Instant Reframe.* Okay, maybe she just came across an article and she wants to share some helpful health tips. I'll ask a gentle question]. Oh, did you see some research recently?

Susan: Yes. It was part of . . .

b) Defending

The second Listening Blocker, defending, is a pattern that comes up automatically because our emotional brain constantly seeks to avoid loss. And our reptile brain guards our survival.

Even a phone conversation can give rise to intense feelings from both the emotional brain and reptile brain. For example, one of my friends pummels people with his rigid viewpoint. Out of shear necessity, I've learned to quiet down my initial defensive reaction. I've learned a method I call *Replace with Relaxation.* So when I return this friend's phone call, I relax in an easy chair before I place the call. During the call, I deep breathe. When I'm in a relaxed space, I can respond to this friend's comments with a neutral phrase "Maybe so."

Replace with Relaxation builds on a process of using one's Observer Mind.

When you go into the Observer Mind, you look at a situation from "a quiet place in yourself." Instead of taking something personally and reacting with anger, you take a deep breath and merely observe it. You begin by taking some deep, slow breaths and let them out slowly. Traditionally, people learn deep breathing by breathing in through the nose and then breathing out through the mouth. This is said to prevent hyperventilation.

Now, in a relaxed state of being, you observe your thoughts as if from a quiet perspective—the Observer Mind. If someone says a hurtful remark, you can pause and step back from it.

Being in the Observer Mind is an advantage. People tend to be in the Ego Mind, which feels vulnerable. When in the Ego Mind, we take things personally and tend to quickly react. But in the Observer Mind, we can merely observe a situation and then *respond*. To respond is to deliberately choose an action—usually one that comes from a calm place.

As you deep breathe and merely observe someone's remark, you can then let your initial defensive reaction stay quiet. Even when you stand up for yourself, it's better to respond.

For example, I coached a client, Nina, to deep breathe and respond. She faced a predicament of an insurance company that was shortchanging her parents. I coached her to deep breathe and prepare a series of comments including, "You need to do better than that" for her next call with the insurance company. She said to the insurance representative, "You need to do better than that" in a calm, relaxed tone. She gained an additional $300 for her parents related to the damage to their car.

c) "Me, too—one up"

This third Listening Blocker is a pattern that sounds like: "You have four classes. That's rough. I have five classes." Many of us have been taught that a way to express concern is to show how we're in a similar situation. But then a bit of ego leaks in and we "one up" the person. Here's another example: "A cracked tooth! Ow! That's awful. Just awful! I've got a dentist's appointment myself next week—root canals. Three of them."

That's not what the other person wants to hear. Why? It trivializes their pain and one seems to be saying: "Look at me. I'm stronger than you. Pity me more!"

When someone is telling you their woes, they just want you to listen. And let *them* feel their feelings. Don't cut them off. And they don't want you to take the conversation spotlight away and talk about *your* problems.

Offer a *Reflective Response.* You reflect back to the person what they are feeling. You can say something like: "That sounds [frustrating, disappointing, tough to endure]." You'll be surprised how fast the person replies, "Yeah. Damn frustrating . . ." And they continue talking and expressing their feelings. They do not even notice that you used a method to reflect their feelings.

How to Remember the Elements of Effective Listening

The mnemonic device of *Observe-Reflect-Ask* can help you during a conversation.

1) *Observe* your own feelings and deep breathe so that you

relax and avoid reacting to someone's comment.

2) *Reflect* the person's feelings back to them by saying something like: "That sounds frustrating."

3) *Ask* a gentle question to ensure the conversation spotlight remains on the other person.

Observe-Reflect-Ask forms the foundation of helping the other person feel heard. When you *Reflect* the person's feeling back to them, they realize that you heard more than their words, you heard their feelings.

When you *Ask* a relevant question, you demonstrate that you paid attention and that you care. A pattern with a gentle question sounds like:

- That sounds frustrating. What happened next?
- That sounds disappointing. Is there some way I can help?
- Wow. That was tough thing to go through. Would you like me to brainstorm some ideas with you – or just keep listening?

It takes practice and rehearsal to learn to listen well. Also, repeated rehearsal forms new neural pathways in your brain. That's important because under stress we tend to fall back on our brain's previous conditioning. So start training to be a great listener.

- **Secret #5: No excuses! Learn to listen!**
- **Your Countermeasure:**

Observe your personal reaction to someone's comment. Quiet down any internal defensive reaction. Then, provide a *Reflective Response* like: "That sounds frustrating." Ask a gentle question. In this way, help the person to feel that he or she is heard.

SECRET #6: YOUR RATIONAL BRAIN DOES THE *TALKING*, BUT THEIR EMOTIONAL BRAIN DOES THE *LISTENING*.

Everybody can be great...because anybody can serve. You don't have to have a college degree to serve. You don't have to make your subject and verb agree to serve. You only need a heart full of grace. A soul generated by love. —Martin Luther King Jr.

In our dinner gathering, Martin Luther King, Jr. raised our level of conversation. A corollary topic came up: What does it take to be a *great* communicator?

Many of us want a personal brand that includes "good leader" or "excellent with people" or "vital member of the team." We want others to understand us, and carry out instructions. Just as we want our co-workers on the same page. This doesn't always happen. Having a reputation for making it happen creates trust and respect. Getting it means facing an age-old conundrum, one inherent in the way human nervous systems work. A problem plaguing every single attempt at communication on all levels and with every individual person is, simply, *talking* and *listening* use different parts of the brain.

Many people think persuading is about saying the right things. Let's look deeper. First, realize that when speaking, you use your neocortex, the top part of your brain devoted to rational thinking. But when someone listens, the person uses his or her *reptile brain* to do it.

The neocortex deals with reason, logic, finding patterns. You use it in organizing your DVD collection or filling out a form. When composing an email message, balancing your checkbook, installing software—the neocortex does what you need. A lot of formal education ends up designed to help train you in using that part of your brain.

But it isn't what you listen with. Our reptile brains don't analyze for the purpose of understanding nor doing an abstract calculation. Rather, that part of the stuff inside our skulls aims for a much more narrow agenda: Survival.

Closely related to the reptile brain is what we call the emotional brain. It too has a single, intense focus: Avoiding loss.

So already, you're in a situation of "disconnect." You're talking from the neocortex and they're listening from the reptile and emotional brains.

A speaker suggests a course of action, offering logical reasons. A listener's brain—the emotional brain—immediately looks for any threat that the listener may lose something. Notice the difference in priority here. The speaker offers reasons to do something. The Listener instantly looks for a reason *not* to do it. Nor is this a matter of individual character or personality. Rather, the part of the brain that listens just does it that way. Reverse the roles of those involved—let the speaker listen and the listener speak—and the identical process takes place.

Then, at the same time, the listener's reptile brain focuses on survival. If any part of the speaker's words appears to threaten the person's survival—in any way at all, no matter how vague—then the reptile part of the brain wants to shut the system down. In effect, that part of the brain will try to get the listener to stop listening.

How do we line up what we say with the listener's emotional and reptile brains? One method is to make a plan to **"speak in headlines"** that *appeal* to the listener's emotional and reptile brains.

To speak in headlines means that you alert the person to the topic, but more than that, you provide an emotional hook.

We're all familiar with news broadcasts that provide a hook before the commercial. The anchorperson says something like: "A new virus is attacking computers. Yours could be next." Now, such a "headline" grabs the listener with both fear of loss (a computer that needs to be replaced) and for home-based business owners, a threat to their financial survival (appealing to their reptile brain).

How Do You Craft a "Headline"?

We'll use what I call the *3 Circles Process*. Pull out a sheet of paper and draw three circles. Label one as "Speaker's Rational Brain." Then label the next two circles consecutively as "Listener's Emotional Brain (Avoid Loss)" and "Listener's Reptile Brain" (Ensure Survival).

How does this work? Here's an example that actually took place at a colleague's office. Management gave an order that everyone should use the same wall clock when signing in and out of breaks.

So picture **Circle #1: Management's Rational Brain** had reasons of streamlining the work process.

However, the workers resisted the change.

Now picture **Circle #2: Workers' Emotional Brain (Avoid Loss):** People actually felt threatened on some level, as if going along with this was a tacit admission of guilt, or they didn't want to give up the independence of using their own timepieces.

Imagine **Circle #3: Workers' Reptile Brain (Ensure Survival):** Workers viewed changing their routine as potentially dangerous on a visceral level. Some said that they were concerned. "What if I make a mistake?" "What if management is double-checking to the minute for each break?"

So what could have been the solution? Management could have presented the change in routine to have emotional benefits for the team like: a) your co-workers will feel better because they'll know when you're out of the office and when they can count on you to return and cover the phone and b) we'll better serve the customers, which will keep us on track and with continued good sales we can avoid seasonal layoffs.

The Next Step is to Craft the Headline:

Here is a possible headline: "Team, we have a small change in the routine. This will help us avoid co-workers getting frustrated about when people get back from breaks. And more importantly, this will help us serve the clients well, which looks like we can avoid seasonal layoffs."

Can you see how "avoid seasonal layoffs" ties directly into the workers' emotional and reptile brains' concerns?

How does this work when talking with one's supervisor?

Remember, you do well by starting a conversation with a "headline." To Frank, her supervisor, Judy says, *"Frank, I think maybe I've found a way to get ourselves a larger budget next year."* This seizes Frank's attention because Judy may help him avoid loss and increase his chances of survival. Often departments fight over funding. Providing a good reason to increase Frank's budget helps Frank protect his little "kingdom"—his department and his job.

How to engage a co-worker in your plan:

Trina says to a co-worker, *"Cara, I have an idea how we can strengthen our position here. Maybe even get ourselves a bonus."* Cara gives Trina her full attention.

This process of crafting a compelling headline that appeals to your listener's emotional and reptile brains will give you an edge in business.

So before you present an idea to a co-worker or supervisor, use the 3 Circles Process and then Craft Your Headline.

The above steps work so well because they take into account human beings' tendency to "thin-slice" when making decisions. Let's explore the elements of "thin-slicing" . . .

Make A Plan to Use "Thin-slicing" to Get What You Want

This next section deals with ideas I first mentioned in my book *Darkest Secrets of Making A Pitch for the Film and Television Industry.*

At this point, I'm going to provide you with some of the background research and information that is "behind the curtain" and underlines how *using the 3 Circles Process and Craft a Headline* prove so valuable.

In his classic book *Blink,* Malcolm Gladwell noticed that people made quick, intuitive decisions as opposed to cautious, deliberate ones. More, they based decisions on something he referred to as "thin-slicing." Of all the information available, people took just a "thin-slice" of it, that is, a quick precis or first impression they received. Then they made a quick decision—one that settled in their minds and wasn't going anywhere.

Near the end of the book, Gladwell wrote of unfair decisions made when people audition for orchestras. If the selection committee saw a woodwind player was a woman, they tended to reject her application. Perhaps they based the rejection on the supposition that a woman with a smaller frame has less lung capacity. Gladwell also described a solution: Have all auditions take place with a screen between the musician and the selection committee, so the musician's gender would not enter the equation. This process would insure fairness.

Why am I sharing this material with you? Because your clients and co-workers will act in a similar manner. When speaking, you're up against that human habit to thin-slice and make a quick, usually permanent, decision. As every conversation begins, unconscious judgments bubble up in the listener's mind. He's nervous, probably trying to put one over on me.

Look at the way this guy is dressed! She looks weak. Wait—what did they just say? Are they kidding me? This one doesn't know the answers to any questions! That nervous tick—he's hiding something.

Of course what you hope for—what you should be aiming for—are different snap judgments. I like him. She sounds confident. I bet this will be a valuable project. He looks me in the eye, so he's honest. She knows what she's talking about. Wow, she didn't even blink—she is calm and forthright.

Gladwell referred to a term for such instant judgments and quick decision-making. He called it *rapid cognition.* It helps to remember rapid cognition is the listeners' tendency to make quick, permanent judgments based on very little data.

This relates to the emotional brain and reptile brain. When you present an effective personal brand, you quiet down the listener's emotional and reptile brains. How? You present a well-crafted headline, one that you built from your use of the 3 Circles Process.

The successful person seizes attention and comes across as confident, honest, competent and forthright. Again, you do that with a well-crafted headline that appeals to the emotional and reptile brains.

The Additional Power You Have When Using a Well-Crafted Headline

When you address directly the concerns of the emotional brain and reptile brain, you inspire something researchers call "wanting" in a person.

Let's look at the above examples' headlines and I'll supply the associated "wanting."

- *"Team, we have a small change in the routine. This will help us avoid co-workers getting frustrated about when people get back from breaks. And more importantly, this will help us serve the clients well, which looks like we can avoid seasonal layoffs."* [Mirna wants a co-worker to stop giving her trouble about when she gets back from a break. Mirna also wants to avoid seasonal layoffs because she's the newest employee and likely to be cut first.]

- *"Frank, I think maybe I've found a way to get ourselves a larger budget next year."* [Frank *wants* his job to be safe so he wants his budget to be larger and his department to be perceived as more important. He also *wants* to "beat" his fellow managers, which stems from pain he still retains from bad treatment during his high school years. Frank wants to feel like a winner.]
- *"Cara, I have an idea how we can strengthen our position here. Maybe even get ourselves a bonus."* [Cara *wants* her job to be safe. Cara also *wants* a bonus so she can get her son a new computer for his homework.]

Now, we have the full process:

a) 3 Circles [Speaker's Rational Brain; Listener's Emotional Brain (Avoid Loss); and Listener's Reptile Brain (Ensure Survival)]
b) Craft a Headline
c) Write down the Listener's Wants
d) Double-check that your headline fits with the Listener's Wants

With enough practice, you'll be able to do the full process quickly in your head while you're on your feet.

When you develop "wanting" in the person, you'll guide them to cooperate and to often say "yes." Remember, they're going to thin-slice and use rapid cognition. Make a plan to get them on your side.

• Secret #6: Your rational brain does the talking but their emotional brains does the listening.

- **Your Countermeasure:**

Remember that people "thin-slice." Use the full process of

a) 3 Circles [Speaker's Rational Brain; Listener's Emotional Brain (Avoid Loss); and Listener's Reptile Brain (Ensure Survival)]
b) Craft a Headline.
c) Write down the Listener's Wants (desires).
d) Double-check that your headline fits with Listener's Wants.

Practice this process on paper and eventually you'll be able to do this in your mind at various points during your day.

SECRET #7: GET SKILLED AT GOOD CONFLICT AND ELIMINATE BAD CONFLICT.

Character cannot be developed in ease and quiet. Only through experience of trial and suffering can the soul be strengthened, ambition inspired, and success achieved. - Helen Keller

The seven notable people seated in our dinner gathering agreed that they needed to develop courage to stand firm during times of conflict and controversy.

Oprah Winfrey said, "Think like a queen. A queen is not afraid to fail. Failure is another steppingstone to greatness."

Helen Keller smiled once her friend and interpreter Anne Sullivan Macy communicated that comment to her.

Martin Luther King, Jr. soon chimed in with: "The ultimate measure of a man is not where he stands in moments of comfort and convenience, but where he stands at times of challenge and controversy."

Some declare that conflict produces good results. Desirable results. Conflict, they say, lies at the heart of competition, forcing us all to strive harder, work longer to find that edge that means winning. It spurs creativity. Separates the best from the merely good. Tempers a business or office the way fire tempers fine steel.

Others say the opposite. Conflict distracts from the main goal. It hinders cooperation, directs energy away from business and towards politics. Nothing, they say, will more likely destroy teamwork or morale than letting conflict in the workplace proceed unchecked.

They both have their points.

Good conflict happens when team members strive to do a great job and they have occasional disagreements. Those disagreements often help. Double-checking ideas often improves them. Finding out how others see things helps develop insight and flexibility.

But bad conflict throws sand into the working gears of your business. It stirs up problems, accomplishes little or nothing, ruins focus, and frequently results from clumsy communication.

I summarize it this way:

Good conflict creates more options.

Bad conflict rises from misunderstandings.

Pause a moment. How are you known at work? For good conflict or bad conflict? Do co-workers look upon you as someone who communicates well and rarely fosters misunderstandings?

With an empowered personal brand, you communicate well. How? Remember your personal brand is your answer to the question: "What are you best known for?"

It helps when your personal brand includes: "trustworthy, tough but fair, coachable, one who listens and who makes improvements, strong and flexible when appropriate."

How does such a personal brand help you communicate well? It helps the other person have a positive or at least neutral disposition toward you. And here's where the good conflict/bad conflict distinction is important. You want to avoid the impression that you're often in the middle of bad conflict with co-workers. That's important because negative impressions stimulate negative emotions that gum up the whole communication process.

Getting Skilled at Good Conflict

In a way, you want to clear the area so good conflict takes place. And you want to avoid situations escalating into turmoil.

1) Avoid Dismissing Ideas Quickly

As I mentioned, good conflict gives you more options. For example, one company was designing a new work space. One person, an introvert, insisted that people needed cubicles and separate offices so they felt some privacy. Another person, an extrovert, said that many of the best ideas arise when workers run into each other during the day and have an off-the-cuff conversation. Both people were adamant in their view. And this conflict related to their personal styles of extrovert and introvert. A concise description of the opposing styles is:

- An extrovert gets energy from being around other people.
- An introvert needs alone time to recover energy.

So whose idea will prevail? The head of the company demonstrated wisdom by not dismissing either idea quickly.

She came up with a plan that incorporated both. The workers had cubicles/offices and a lounge area was placed immediately adjacent to the restrooms. Team members were invited to take a break in the inviting lounge area, which had lots of windows and comfortable chairs with a few tables. Impromptu meetings occurred during the day. If a team member felt stuck, they would bring a laptop to the area and talk with an occasional passerby.

When your personal brand includes: "Someone who listens to unusual ideas" you create more options. You make sure that co-workers feel free to offer up ideas—even hare-brained ones.

To avoid escalating turmoil, be sure you help the other person feel heard. Hear them out even if your gut says, "No. That's so dumb." Keep your mouth shut. Listen. A dumb idea might end up as a springboard for a great one. That's what brainstorming is all about.

Still, the idea may well be useless. And you might know it instantly. Still, don't dismiss the person with that useless idea out of hand. They'll feel it, and they'll resent it. So would almost anyone. Hence, bad conflict, sooner or later. (Besides, this isn't really even fair—we've all come up with bad ideas at one time or another.)

There are two important business considerations that may encourage people to dismiss ideas quickly: a) time and b) a pattern of bad ideas.

Time

Since my team is working with four franchises, we're dealing with multiple deadlines simultaneously. Every day I'm leading projects related to *Crystal Pegasus* (for children); *Jack AngelSword* (fantasy-thriller); *TimePulse* (science fiction) and *"Secrets . . . How to Protect Yourself."* I need to protect my own time and the work time of my team members.

Still, I foster an environment that welcomes ideas. Here's one of my ways to protect time but still respect the person who suggests an idea. Often I respond to ideas with: "Let me think about that for a while" or "I'm not sure yet" and "Thanks for bringing that up." You see that I'm honoring the person by listening first and considering their idea.

A Pattern of Bad Ideas

This situation is trickier because all sorts of other issues come into play, including the quality of what this person does in general and how others react to seeing someone treat stupid ideas with respect.

The real answer relates to true leadership.

As a leader, I foster an environment in which I welcome lots of ideas. I talk with my team members about how Walt Disney would go to his team and ask them to "plus this" (his term for adding something and improving the project).

At the same time, team members know that I'm a stickler for time efficiency. They'll hear me say, "Hmmm. Interesting idea. Let's have you continue with the first two pages of the graphic novel, and I'll take that idea and have a conversation with the art director as soon as I can."

Later, I may share an objection to the idea. I'll say something like: "I've thought about the idea. I'm wondering how business owners in New York will respond to it—because they're an important segment of our target market." So the discussion continues *about the idea* with no insults to the person who proposed the idea.

About "how others react to seeing someone treat stupid ideas with respect":

My goal is to *treat people with respect* and to put ideas through a sorting process. The person will be heard. On the other hand, the idea will be poked and stretched—and used or discarded.

Remember, you can avoid a great deal of bad conflict

when you hear a person out and avoid dismissing an idea too quickly.

2) Hold to a Positive Position . . . with the Possibility of Being Flexible

When I say "Positive Position" I mean that you are holding firm to something you value. The opposite is often heard as something like: "No. I won't do that" or "I'm against paying the standard fee." Instead, you simply and positively state your position. Hold firm. Do not apologize for your situation. Here's an example: I'll say, "We're doing multiple projects and I have a modest budget for this project."

In this way, I'm acknowledging the truth. The fee I'm inviting the vendor to agree to is modest. This is often a business reality. Some companies who do a number of entrepreneurial projects must keep costs down or they won't be able to "keep the lights on" (that is, pay their bills). I've seen over the years that some entrepreneurial projects do well and create a good cash flow. Other projects fail: perhaps, the market was not ready for the product or some other external detail takes place. For example, when the 911 tragedies occurred, many conferences were cancelled, which put a lot of my speaking industry colleagues into a tailspin.

An effective business builds up a reserve of cash and resources. How? By firmly negotiating so that costs per project are modest.

Now, I'll share two phrases that help you maintain your firm positive position:

- *"Can you do better than that?"*

At one point, I was negotiating for some equipment for a film project. The vendor suggested a price. I asked, "Can you do better than that?" Then the vendor went on with some peripheral details. What's the conflict here? She was attempting to ignore my point and overwhelm me with other details. When she completed her comment, I said, "That's not what I said. Can you do better than that?" Then I was silent. I could see that she was a bit uncomfortable, but eventually she named another lower fee amount. And subsequently, we made the deal.

- *"That's not on the table."*

At one point, I was negotiating with a graphic artist to render a cover. This person wanted residuals. Where was the conflict here? It was all about money. My budget was set up to offer a one-time fee. I said, "That's not on the table (referring to residuals)." In this way, I alerted him that we may not have had a match. And that was a good thing because it showed my resolve. I agreed that his work was excellent and that was why I offered him the cover. And still, I remained firm and quite willing to walk away from the potential deal. He did come around to my terms.

Now, I'll share a phrase that implies that one may have a bit of flexibility: *"Are you okay with this?"*

After some spirited negotiation (more about this in my book *Darkest Secrets of Negotiation Masters*), you need to make sure that the other person is okay with the arrangement. Why? Resentful people often sabotage projects—sometimes deliberately and other times unconsciously. Watch the person's face and body language carefully. If you sense that the person feels victimized by the negotiation, consider being flexible on a couple of the details. Ask, "Are you okay with this?" and see if something needs to be adjusted. A useful phrase is: "No deal is better than a bad deal."

Do not shy away from good conflict. Situations stir up difficult feelings. The successful don't avoid this, but they do *manage* it. They practice methods to communicate clearly what they want, and they make space for feelings. After all, those feelings will be there no matter what. Still, they realize that business often requires compromise and someone is likely to end up uncomfortable. What escalates discomfort to the point of resentment and bad conflict is nearly always a sense of *unfair treatment*. No adult expects to always get their way. But co-workers and managers aren't just someone. You are not a stranger to your fellows at work, so they have an emotional investment in your behavior. Hence the need for a personal brand. No one can always be the "nice guy/gal." But a personal brand of "tough but fair" inspires belief and trust. It fosters good conflict and discards the bad. At that point, you have joined the ranks of excellent communicators.

- **Secret #7: Get skilled at good conflict and eliminate bad conflict.**

- **Your Countermeasure:**

Avoid the mistakes that lead to bad conflict (needless turmoil). Get skilled at good conflict including the judicious use of the phrases:

- "Can you do better than that?"
- "That's not on the table."
- "Are you okay with this?"

BOOK TWO: METHODS TO SAVE TIME, REDUCE STRESS AND MAKE MORE MONEY

I am a woman in process. I'm just trying like everybody else. I try to take every conflict, every experience, and learn from it. Life is never dull. - Oprah Winfrey

To make your personal brand as effective as possible take each experience and find how to improve your communication. Your personal brand is a shortcut to getting more done and relating better with business associates. In this section we'll explore three topics:

- Save Time: The S.A.V.E. Process
- Reduce Stress: The L.E.S.S. Process
- Make More Money: The M.O.R.E. Process

Save Time: The S.A.V.E. Process

A good element for your personal brand is: "highly professional, straight-to-the-point." It takes practice to communicate in ways that are clear and save time. We'll use the S.A.V.E. process to guard your precious resource, time:

S - Single out the Crucial Detail

A - Access "What they want"

V - Vocalize feelings

E - Express the "Headline" and add a "Tagline"

1. Single out the Crucial Detail

An essential part of saving time is prioritizing. When a project appears, focus your attention on what is *absolutely essential*. For example, when I decided to do a second edition of one of my books, I had limited time and a limited budget for editors. The previous draft comprised 73,000 words. Immediately, I cut 40,000 words. I knew I'd probably add 10,000 words of new material. My making tough choices helped the project come in on time and under budget.

Now, how does my book coming in on time relate to your personal brand? It's an example of something that I'm best known for: *a leader who gets results.*

As I mentioned earlier in this book, your personal brand begins with your answer to the question: "What are you best known for?" In essence, your personal brand is *a promise of performance.* Assess if you're best known as *someone who gets the most important things done.* Can people count on you to make the tough decisions?

Unfortunately, I often see the opposite: many individuals fail to think things through. They get caught in some distracting detail like trying to have an "ego-win." An ego-win is merely something that will help someone feel good, just to satisfy that person's ego. For example, in my book, *Darkest Secrets of Negotiation Masters,* I note that it is often fruitless to try to get the other side to acknowledge that you were right. Instead, you need to focus on what's most important in any interaction. An ego-win is not as important as getting excellent results.

Before you begin an interaction, take a moment to jot down a couple of notes. Answer these questions:

a) What is most important here?—to me?—to the other person?—to my company?—to my supervisor?
b) What does my ego want? Do I want to be "proven to be right"? (Would that satisfy my ego?) Do I want an apology?
c) What is the Crucial Detail?

Every human interaction is a mini-negotiation. Even just saying hello is a brief give-and-take moment. Just notice how some people will get upset if someone does not reply "hello" when they walk past each other in the hallway.

Often in a negotiation, a change in behavior is most important, not getting someone's acknowledgment that you were right all along.

When I'm talking about the ego-win as not that important, I'm opening the door for what truly is important: **The Crucial Detail.**

The Crucial Detail consists of what is absolutely essential. When you know that, you can save a lot of time by cutting the nonessentials. For example, if you know a report is going to be subsequently modified by two co-workers, do not lose time making the report "perfect." In order to find what is essential, ask your supervisor questions such as: "What do you want to see in this report? . . . What's most important to you that I place in this report?"

2. Access "What they want"

Some time ago, I was working with a co-composer for a film music soundtrack. At one point, I could see that she was irritated in some way. I asked, "What do you want?" Further in the conversation, I asked, "Do you want me to kick myself up to Executive Music Producer and for you to get the credit of Music Producer?"

I have learned to ask "What do you want?" in a gentle and pleasant way. I know that I may not always respond with an answer that pleases the other person, but it saves time to get the information "on the table."

Sometimes, you need to be "fearless." Ask the person to tell you what they want. Know that reality may require that you not give her exactly what she wants, but you come across as strong when you simply ask, "What do you want?" And that helps your personal brand. How? A confident and competent person (that's a good personal brand) is strong enough to face the tough details in business. Further, realize an essential part of your personal brand is: "trustworthy, honest and forthright."

3. Vocalize feelings

Imagine how good someone would feel if they know you understand their point of view. How do you let that person know that you understand? You can say something like: "That sounds frustrating [disappointing, tough to go through]."

The simple truth is: If you do *not* acknowledge someone's feelings as important, they are likely to do something to sabotage your efforts later. Unfortunately, a number of people you're likely to meet quickly categorize people into "villains" and friends. For example, "James" heard that his friend Cindy was frustrated that her supervisor decided against Cindy's raise in salary. James said, "What an a___e!" James does *not* truly know the supervisor or what constraints the supervisor is under. But still, James immediately categorizes the supervisor as "enemy." You'll also how see how fast people categorize people on a freeway as "idiots" or "morons."

My point here is that you enhance your career when you help people feel good in your presence. Make space for their feelings. Acknowledge how they feel.

4. Express the "Headline" and add a "Tagline"

A prime way to save time is to tell people what you mean in bite-sized chunks, in a way that seizes their attention. How? Use the method "Speak in Headlines with Taglines." Authors Lois P. Frankel and Carol Frohlinger write: "[This method helps you get] your point across more effectively and succinctly without coming across as brazen or strident."

We use two steps to speak in headlines with taglines:

1) Identify what your point and recommendation is.
2) Open the discussion up so others may chime in with their ideas and recommendations.

A tagline can be "I'd like to open the discussion up and hear . . ."

In context, the two steps can sound like this:

"I'm concerned that the tree is listing and because two branches have fallen off—the next branch may fall on our neighbor's house. I'd recommend that we have the tree cut down as soon as possible to avoid possible injuries to our neighbors—and a likely lawsuit. These are my thoughts. I'd like to open this discussion up and hear other people's thoughts and recommendations about this."

This method makes your point clear and avoids having people drift off. Let's face it: if people get either confused or bored when you're talking—they don't like it!

To avoid people's resistance, preplan what you're going

to say. You'll save time at that moment in the conversation. And you'll also save time by avoiding future misunderstandings.

REDUCE STRESS: THE L.E.S.S. PROCESS

I'll put it in a few words: our mouths cause us so much needless stress. How? We talk when others need us to listen. We give advice or criticize when others need our support.

Let's take this further. Imagine if your personal brand included: "Good listener." What would result? People would feel comfortable around you and they'd trust you. Research demonstrates that many of the best salespeople are the best listeners. By listening, they get cooperation and their lives go smoother. To reduce stress, we'll use the L.E.S.S. process:

L - Listen
E - Ease up
S - Select Criteria for Excellence
S - Sidestep resistance

1. Listen

I have a relative who couldn't listen to another person if his life depended on it. It's tragic really. This person misses so much of what is warm and genuine in life. And imagine what his family misses, too. This guy only has one friend. He's dropped everyone else. And they're probably saying, "Thank you. Thank you!"

On the other hand, people who listen well often find that people like them and offer them more opportunities.

The central element of listening is restraining yourself from making reactive comments. Pause. See if you can make space for the person to experience what he or she is feeling. How do you "make space"? You don't talk about your reaction to something they said. You acknowledge what they're feeling by saying something as simple as "That sounds frustrating." Often, I hear the other person reply, "Yeah! It *was* frustrating and then . . ."

When we acknowledge the other person's feelings, they have an opportunity to relax—because they feel we're not going to "hijack the conversation" to focus on ourselves. If we do not give the other person space to be heard, then they feel a tension to prove himself or herself right. You reduce stress by listening and thus eliminating such tension.

In the past, one of my elderly relatives denied that I was under pressure. He repeatedly said, "You chose that." That's such a easy comment for my relative to say. People choose things all the time. *But that does nothing to eliminate* that many of our choices are *expensive.* We *pay for* what we want. To choose to have a child means putting your heart through worry, anxiety, and heartache. Parenthood is tough. But imagine how cruel it would be to say, "You chose having a kid" when a mother runs to a hospital to attend her dying teenager.

Many of us would realize that saying something heartless to a distraught mother is inappropriate. But there are smaller pressures that we may miss.

If someone complains about some tough (but less intense) situation, it helps your relationship with them when you say: "That sounds rough. How did things go for you?"

2. Ease up

Some people try too hard at whatever activity they're engaged in. You can see them straining. On the other hand, the best actors "make it look easy." How do they do that?

Many of them *have trained in methods to develop relaxation* on stage or before a movie camera.

Similarly, I have trained myself in ways to relax for giving a pitch, that is, presenting a proposed film to investors or studio executives. In my book *Darkest Secrets of Making A Pitch for Film and Television,* I write about one of my relaxation methods: I tell myself: "Let's see if they want to play." That's part of my process to ease up. I've trained myself to use certain words, *want to play,* to transform my perception of the pitching session.

The idea of "want to play" brings the interaction out of the emotional brain's perception of "life or death."

Another part of "ease up" is to relax and let the other person say what he or she needs to say first. When two people meet and talk, each one wants to express personal thoughts and feelings. When you let the other person go first, you eliminate tension. Then the person is likely to be more receptive to hearing you. This process reduces stress for both you and the other person.

3. Select Criteria for Excellence

Being a perfectionist is stressful! I know this because I have often tried to "be perfect" in how I treat each person with whom I come in contact. I try to be so compassionate and kind to everyone I meet. But sometimes I fall short because I'm distracted. There is a solution: instead of aiming for perfection, aim for excellence. What is excellence? You decide. Set up your own *Criteria for Excellence.* For example, I train my graduate students in my public speaking class to focus on this idea: *"We don't need you to be perfect; we do need you to be genuine."* When you aim to be a real human being and express some truth (at least something that is true to you), you can take some of the pressure off yourself. How?

Tell yourself that it's okay to make small mistakes and to "be human" in front of your audience and that lightens your load. You realize that you do not need to pronounce each word perfectly to get your message across. Instead, you focus on talking to the audience—and *not* at them.

Here's another imperfect moment for any presenter: the instant one's mind goes blank. If your mind goes blank, you can say, "I'll need a moment. My brain needs more RAM." And then the audience (at least in Silicon Valley) will enjoy the human moment and the humor.

4. Sidestep resistance

Resistance and conflict cause more and more stress in business interactions. What if you could avoid needless resistance? How would your life improve?

Here's the big opportunity. Add this to your personal brand: "effective storyteller." How do you avoid a lot of needless resistance? Tell a vivid, to-the-point story.

Do not start by making some biased, blanket statement (such as "all workers in the blue room have it tough"). Instead, *tell a story*. Give the audience (which can be one co-worker or a group in a room) an *experience*. Tell what you learned. It helps to end your story with something like: "So that day, I learned to pay attention to the little things because they can really trip you up—if you're not careful."

You can really reduce your stress, when you focus on these 4 elements:

L - Listen

E - Ease up

S - Select Criteria for Excellence

S - Sidestep resistance

MAKE MORE MONEY: THE M.O.R.E. PROCESS

To make money, you need to communicate well with other people. And you need to communicate effectively *with yourself.* What does that mean? It means that all day long you're, in effect, talking to yourself. Sometimes, we even see someone say bits of *self-talk* out loud, particularly when they're frustrated. They might exclaim, "Stupid! Stupid!" and they're referring to themselves.

To communicate well to yourself means to change your habits of self-talk. Stop cutting yourself down. Instead of saying "Stupid!," tell yourself, "I made an error. I can do better." Start focusing on crucial details, set appropriate goals, and develop empowering habits.

I have developed empowering habitual thought patterns. For example, I tell myself that *I do not delay.* This phrase is helpful for me. In one year and two months, I completed nine writing projects that resulted in nine published books available on Amazon.com. How did I do that? I *monetized* an idea, gathered a team, communicated clearly with them and led them to complete the projects. At times, I had three editors working on one book simultaneously. I'd write in the morning and then send material from section one to Editor #1. Later, I'd finish section two and send that material to Editor #2.

Let's take a closer look at *monetizing.* Author Marziah Karch writes: "*Monetize* means to convert something to money. In Internet terms monetize refers to finding a way to generate income from items posted on the Web. Web sites are usually monetized by either selling ad space or creating a related product line, such as T-shirts with slogans."

Monetizing begins with an idea. I first start with something good I want to do for other people. For example, the impetus for my book *Darkest Secrets of Making a Pitch for Film and Television* was my desire to save new filmmakers from suffering when they start pitching to other people. I began that book with these words:

"This is the book I wish existed when I began in the film industry. Do you have a movie you want to make? So did I. Or a screenplay that you want produced? Me, too. Are you going to pitch a project to a studio executive, producer, name actor or private investor? I've made many pitches. But back then I didn't know how and I hit wall after wall. It felt like a blow to the stomach at the time. In fact, I felt so much uncertainty and pain that I found myself avoiding the whole situation. I would stay up too late at night rewriting a screenplay, sleep all day, and *lose* that day when I needed to be out looking for funding. Perhaps you can relate to that.

"The good news is you can *avoid* feeling stuck. Now, through this book, I will be your coach. Much of this material builds on my observations of dire mistakes, my own and others'. After successfully gaining funding for a number of projects and international distribution (one film went to the Cannes film market), I have compiled what worked.

"I've seen other filmmakers give presentations that crashed and burned. So I'm inspired to provide you with the means to achieve your dream."

So the above was my introduction to my book on pitching. Now, I could take that same information and give a guest presentation to another college instructor's class. I'd serve about 20 students at that time. And I'd feel good to be at the service of those few students.

But that's putting a limit on how many people I can serve

at one time. (By the way, this relates to the big limit of being paid by the hour. You can only make money when you're literally at work.) So how could I take this useful knowledge and truly monetize it? The first step is to find a venue for selling the material that has *no* ceiling, that is *no* limit—and Amazon.com is such a venue. I know how to prepare an ebook and place it into the Amazon.com system—and it's posted on the Amazon.com website in less than three hours.

Here's an important element of monetizing an idea. See if you can do the work once and then have an income stream that requires no more work on your part. When I write books and have Amazon.com do the selling and mailing, I've done the work only once. And I have literally been sleeping while my books were being purchased.

Now that I've shared one example with the above ebook, let's get specific with the M.O.R.E. process.

M - Monetize what you're already doing

O - Open the possibilities on modest budgets

R - Request a response

E - Enroll

1. Monetize what you're already doing

Some brilliant people I know do amazing things, but they fail to convert what they're doing into ways to make money. Why? For one thing, they never received training in monetizing ideas.

You can find ways to take what you're already doing and make such activities into an income stream. For example, today I called a friend and shared my idea of how he could monetize what he's already doing. Currently, he interviews book authors for his own internet radio show.

Here's something he can decide to do:

1) Choose authors that have something to teach

people.

2) Ask specific questions so that the author can teach his listeners a skill.
3) Go to Fiverr.com and get someone to take the recordings of the interviews and make written transcripts.
4) Combine the transcripts into a new ebook for Amazon's Kindle.

The above is one example that demonstrates that one can take current activities and add an element that brings new value to others—and profits to your pocket.

2. Open the possibilities on modest budgets

One way to make more money is to have products that are earning money while you're doing something else. But there's a problem: Which entrepreneurial project is going to break through? Which one will yield good profits? You'll never know until a product gets into the marketplace. How can you afford to experiment? I've learned from experience that it's often necessary to keep multiple projects to modest budgets to open the possibilities for profit.

It's best to keep costs down because one has no assurance that any particular project will break even, let alone make good profits. It takes skill to keep budgets modest. Recently, one of my colleagues asked, "How do you get a good rate from vendors, Tom?"

I explained the process I used. It's outlined below:

Tell the truth.

Consider saying something like: "I'm doing multiple projects and each has a limited budget. So this time I'm going to have to ask you for the 'friend rate.' I'm sad that I can't offer more. I'm hoping that we can come up with something so you'll say: 'This is okay.'"

You can continue with: "I'd prefer that at some point, I can bring a project to you with a fee level that you'd say: 'This is great!' But at the moment, with the number of projects I'm doing, I can only offer you something that you can be 'okay' with. So what fee will you be okay with?"

It takes courage to ask for lower rates. But the truth is an entrepreneur rides a roller coaster. Some projects yield nothing. Other projects create a good cash flow. You need to be strategic about your costs.

Some people feel embarrassed about having a modest budget and asking for lower rates. Years ago, when I needed to ask for lower rates, I bolstered my own feelings when I realized that I had helped people earn money to pay for their rent and their healthcare costs—even when my own income was limited. So even if you offer only "okay" fees, you're still doing something good: providing people with work and you're making progress.

3. Request a response

To get a person to buy your product or hire you, you need for them to engage *with you*. And the person needs to interact with what you're demonstrating. You need to connect with their emotions. Top salespeople the world over have noted: *People buy on emotion and later justify on facts.* So if you want someone to buy your product or hire you, you need to develop "wanting" in that person. And that "wanting" must be stronger than the person's natural resistance and fear. I'm using the word *wanting* with care because a number of researchers have identified the term *wanting* as an element that occurs quickly in a conversation if the salesperson or persuader is skillful.

How do you do develop wanting in the buyer? Tell an

effective story. Share with the person how someone like them benefited from your product or service. This relates to the principle: *Stories sell; facts just tell.*

How do you know which story to tell? You ask the person gentle questions. What are gentle questions? They're the opposite of harsh questions that put a person on the spot. A harsh question sounds like: "Wouldn't you feel ashamed if you didn't buy a top line computer for your son?"

On the other hand, a gentle question would sound like: "So how do you see your son doing well with this computer?"

Here's an example:

Sarah: So what's most important to you?—expressing yourself creatively or financial security?

Mark: Financial security.

Sarah: How is that going for you?

Mark: In the current economic recession, my business is down by 19%.

Sarah: Oww. That hurts.

Mark: You're damn right.

Sarah: If I could show you how to increase your sales by 37%, would that be interesting to you?

Mark: Sure.

Sarah: Let me tell about George Smydell's experience . . . (and Sarah tells a triumphant story).

Good questions, good listening and good stories help you make more money.

4. Enroll

To enroll someone, you need them to take action and to make a commitment. You need to ask for the sale. No product or service "sells itself."

How can you efficiently get the person to say “yes”?

First, make it easy.

Do not say, “Sign here.” The phrase “sign here” raises alarm bells. Some people think of “signing my life away.” That is, they’re afraid of getting into a deal that can cripple them financially.

Instead, say, “So, now you can ’okay’ this.” And then place the paperwork in front of them and give them a pen.

Related to enrolling people, I’ll share a method from my book *Be Heard and Be Trusted.*

Here’s a method with which to end a pitch:

"Because of [Reason #1] and [Reason #2], I encourage you to say ’yes’ to my project.”

The above statement includes four elements that really work:

1) You’re forthright. Your tone and precise language convey that you believe in what you’re offering.

2) You use the magic word “because.” Research demonstrates that people (at least in the continental United States) expect that a logical reason to take action follows the word “because.”

3) You’ve mentioned two reasons that mean something to your client. (How do you know that? You’ve listened carefully and now you’re repeating their reasons that you’ve discovered along the way.)

4) You put the word “yes” into the room. I have seen people respond with nodding their head after I put the word “yes” into the room. (I also nod my head and a number of people tend to subconsciously follow along.)

In my work with clients and graduate students in teaching them to effectively pitch their projects, I see that rehearsing effective methods (like those above) gets great results. Using my coaching, one of my students won a Charles Schwab scholarship.

And what did I just do with the previous sentence? I shared with you a one-sentence 'story': *Using my coaching, one of my students won a Charles Schwab scholarship.*

How is this a story? I imply that my student trained with me and earned the triumphant ending of winning a Charles Schwab scholarship.

You see, stories do not have to be long-winded. Just get used to making your points by giving examples.

Develop your own stories and rehearse methods to enroll people in what you're offering. Always remember: ask for the sale and ask for the order.

And then, you're on your way to making more money.

BOOK THREE: IMPROVE YOUR BUSINESS COMMUNICATION

One can never consent to creep when one feels an impulse to soar. - Helen Keller

To soar in making our dreams come true, we need to improve how we communicate. When we talk about the *Secrets of Business Communication,* it helps to explore some essential methods of vivid and respectful communication. Earlier, I emphasized that adapting to people's emotions is essential. Now, we'll explore five topics to improve your skills and keep your business interactions positive:

1) Beware the "Double-Slap" — a Big Mistake in Business
2) How Do You Win an Argument?
3) Do You Know the Top 3 Career Crippling Mistakes?
4) Find Your Power to Make a Tough Speech During an Economic Recession
5) How Can You Get Someone to Say "Yes"?

1) Beware the "Double-Slap" — a Big Mistake in Business

Ever open your email browser, then open an email message — and SLAP, someone's words knock you down flat?

You've been hit by what I call the Double-Slap.

First, the person is saying "No" to you (slap) and second, it's through email (slap #2). Ugh.

So it hurts to be on the receiving end of a Double-Slap. Hence, I advise avoiding the practice yourself. If you have to say "no," pick up a phone. That is, if you want to maintain the business relationship. And it's not just the word "no." It can be anything unpleasant. For example, you could moderately complain that you have been waiting for someone's reply email message. But the person could interpret the complaint as an insult about his professionalism.

Using the phone is better than an email because, when you call on the phone, your voice and tone can soften the experience of tough news for the listener. Also, in the moment, you can clear up any misunderstanding and avoid an email "flame war."

Email can cause trouble. The truth is: we have no idea how a person is feeling when they open our email message. The person may be viewing your message at 1 AM after a fight that day with the spouse or boss. Or how about if their spouse is their boss?

That's why I often begin a message with "Thank you for . . ."

Why?

Because I ask you: "Are we just thanked too much for our

efforts?"

No.

I like to express appreciation. And I appreciate being appreciated. Don't you?

I put my best effort forward. And you do, too—right? It's high time someone thanked you. By the way, thank you for reading this book.

What do you do if you've been Double-Slapped?

It's a temptation to respond—or react—immediately to an email that bothers us. I've made the mistake to immediately call the person. Bad move. By definition, a Double-Slap hurts. It can knock you off balance.

Instead, take time to calm down. Perhaps, debrief with a trusted friend.

Take six minutes to, perhaps, close your eyes and deep breathe while expanding your belly (belly-breathing).

Get a lot of practice in learning to calm yourself down. For example, I carry a timer so I can meditate on a train or plane.

After you've taken time to calm down, then jot down some notes about how you can gently and reasonably respond to the bothersome email. And better yet, rehearse your calm response with a trusted friend before you make that phone call to the Double-Slapper.

To rehearse, you could pick up your cell phone and call your friend.

What if you don't want to disturb a friend? Call your own answering system, and record your rehearsal. My clients tell me that it feels like "showtime" when they record their rehearsal.

If you have to say "no" or express unpleasant news, pick

up a phone and avoid doing a Double-Slap via email. Your tone of voice can soften the tough experience for the listener. It's even better if you can talk in-person when you have disappointing news for someone.

Just a little more consideration means better relationships. It's worth it.

Some Thoughts about "Beware the 'Double-Slap'—a Big Mistake in Business" and Your Personal Brand

Imagine the trouble that comes from a personal brand of "that person is cold." What's the problem? Many people naturally avoid talking about difficulties with someone they find to be cold and emotionally distant. And they don't trust such a cold person. This can cause big trouble in business. In order to do our job well, we need to hear about trouble fast—so we can fix a problem.

Further, in the current economic recession, people are deeply concerned about holding on to a job. How do you protect your job? Many of us play our cards close to the vest. We do *not* want to be vulnerable. So we keep our interactions with cold people to a minimum.

On the other hand, we want an effective personal brand that conveys our competence and trustworthiness. So it's best if you have cordial interactions with co-workers, your supervisor and clients. Continue to ensure that your personal brand includes "friendly, efficient and competent." To keep interactions positive, use the phone (when possible) instead of email to convey disappointing information. People still find that talking in person conveys a warm, personal touch.

2) HOW DO YOU WIN AN ARGUMENT?

Just two words.

Really?

Yes–but they're two tough words to say in the heat of the moment.

Are you ready?

"You're right."

You may respond, "But the other person is wrong. And it's not appropriate to agree with their point."

You're right.

Okay, now it may seem that saying these two words is too simple—and you're right about that. My point (which I learned from the work of Dr. David D. Burns) is that we enhance our business relationship by acknowledging just a kernel of how the other person has a correct point or idea.

Acknowledging how the other person is right can sound like:

"You're right. I crossed the line. I didn't mean to bring up the lost client again. It sounds like you're upset about how I talked to the graphic designer, do I have that about right?"

Do you see what's going on here? You've stopped your own behavior of pushing back. You've acknowledged how the other person may be feeling. But you are not telling the person how he feels. You end with a question that acknowledges that you could be wrong in your guess about what he feels.

The pattern: "You're right . . . I made the mistake of . . . It sounds like . . . Do I have that about right?"—takes practice.

But here's a secret. It works like a miracle.

I have friendships that have lasted as long as 26 years. One of the reasons those friendships have blossomed is I admit my errors.

How do you win an argument?

You get past your own ego.

Basically, you're replacing an argument with a conversation that fosters connection. Such a conversation begins with "You're right."

I didn't say it was easy.

It takes rehearsal.

Rehearsal helps you re-condition your brain. The good news is our brain has *neuroplasticity*, that means we can mold the brain to have better responses. And we all have a lot of conditioning to reprogram.

You might say: "That would take a bit of time."

You're right.

Some Thoughts about "Saying 'You're Right'" or Admitting an Error —and Your Personal Brand

When your personal brand is "trustworthy person," you have no ceiling in how successful you can become. People enjoy offering you opportunities. Business interactions go faster and smoother. On the other hand, without trust, people clog the system with self-defensive tactics and actions.

When I work with someone who can admit an error, I felt at ease. Why? Because I know that things are likely to go well and there will be *no hiding of errors* that can cause big problems later. Here's an example of hiding errors: During the production of James Cameron's feature film *Titanic* a member of the production concealed unpaid bills in a drawer that totaled, according to some reports, over $1 million. The production had not paid these bills so in essence the film was about $1 million over budget. When these unpaid bills were discovered, Cameron faced *even more pressure* from the studio about cost overruns for the massive film production!

The idea of *no hiding of errors* relates to a good personal brand. Someone with an effective personal brand is known for having finesse when dealing with people. When you can smoothly admit errors, you counteract the problem that people hate arrogant co-workers, the ones who never admit errors and never give credit where credit is due. When you and I say to someone, "You're right," we're affirming the other person's intelligence and diligence. We're making a friend.

So build up your own ego strength. Learn to say, in a forthright manner, "You're right" or "I made an error." Some time ago, one of my contractors asked, "Did my check go into the mail on Monday?" I immediately replied, "I made an error. I'll total your project fees and write the check within the next 20 minutes." [It was 12:30 AM and I was intending to wind down for sleep.] I continued, "And I'll send you an email confirming the amount. And one of my team members will get your check to the post office tomorrow." Only later in the conversation did I identify the unusual circumstances that led to my error—that is, my oversight. But you see that I did *not* defend myself first. Instead, I provided the solution immediately. This method of responding is all about maintaining people's trust—the basis of your effective personal brand.

3) DO YOU KNOW THE TOP 3 CAREER CRIPPLING MISTAKES?

What do you procrastinate on? Taxes paperwork? Well, who doesn't?

But three particular and big mistakes can cripple your career:

1. Putting off networking

I know someone who is terrific at what she does. But she doesn't keep her resume updated. She doesn't attend industry events. She's not on LinkedIn.com nor is she in Facebook. She's not on Twitter. A blog? – forget it.

Now, I realize that some of us don't feel that we have an easy way with words. But I have a question for you: Who knows you? And who knows that you're an expert at what you do?

A couple of years ago, I saw the phrase: "It's not who you know; it is who knows you."

Unfortunately, many of us hesitate to do networking activities because we feel uncomfortable about asking people for things. No wonder. Instead, I invite you to focus on a secret of networking: *Help other people first.* Many people will naturally want to return a favor. And this becomes a healthy and enjoyable way to live: sharing resources and leads—and creating a circle of support.

How do you create a circle of support? Become a benevolent detective, that is, find ways to be supportive of your new acquaintances. What's the fastest way to learn how you can help someone? Ask this question: "How can I be supportive of what you're doing?"

The Solution to Overcome Career Crippling Mistake #1:

How do you make sure to do some networking efforts each day? Get a timer. I invite you to do something (send an email, send an invitation for connecting on Linkedin.com, reply to a comment on Facebook, make a phone call) to connect with more people for 15 minutes a day. A daily 15 minutes will—in one year's time—add up to 91 hours.

A simple thing you can do is send a thank-you note to someone in your circle who has provided some support for you. Perhaps the person sent you a link to an article related to your industry. You can express appreciation for any kindness.

Networking takes time. I realize that attending an industry event can take an evening. For the week in which you attend an event, give yourself credit—and perhaps, you might choose to limit your other networking efforts on other days of that week.

On the other hand, I tend to do networking efforts nearly every day. For example, yesterday I made three calls to talk with references for a new intern. Within 20 minutes, I invited all three managers to connect to me on Linkedin.com, and they did.

The process of networking is like feeding a baby. We need to be consistent about it!

2. Failure to make it fun and easy to help you

"There are no self-made millionaires." I came across these words so long ago. To leap forward, we all need leads—leads to a job or prospective clients. And many of us have a significant other or spouse because of being connected through friends. In essence, we gained a "lead" to a suitable spouse.

We all need to use tact. If you haven't talked with

someone for years but then learn that they work at a furniture store . . . it is *not* appropriate to ask that the person help you with his employee discount. Why? You have no relationship with the person and it's simply tactless to ask for such a favor. (I actually read that someone tried the premature asking for the favor—and, of course, failed.)

Instead, reconnect first.

The Solution to Overcome Career Crippling Mistake #2:

How do you make it fun and easy for someone to help you? Listen to that person first.

Isn't it true that we all need a supportive listener? Even for five minutes. How do we set things up so we're listening fast? At a networking event, ask gentle questions and listen. What are gentle questions? These are questions that are open-ended and give people the chance to talk about things that are fun for them:

- What are you looking forward to?
- What's one of your favorite movies?
- What are your hobbies?
- What's something good that's happened for you in the recent couple of weeks?

The Law of Reciprocity is an observation that many people will want to help you after you have been helpful or kind to them first. Sure, not all people return favors. But I know a guy who is always helping someone—some assistance he gets paid for and some assistance he doesn't. But helping is his lifestyle. And people offer him opportunities and referrals. It makes his life easier and more fun.

3. Failure to ask

What do you lose if you do not ask? You took the chance

to jump up to the next level of success. When you ask the right people in the right way for the right thing, your career success expands.

But fear stops many of us. I have felt it, too. Years ago, I hesitated to ask for a particular person's endorsement for a book I was working on. Then a supportive friend said, "You don't have the endorsement now. And if the person says 'no'—you still won't have the endorsement. What changed?"

Now, that's a good question!

Back then, I had to do some soul searching. I soon realized that, probably on a subconscious level, I was afraid that I would lose in some ways:

- I'd lose some good feelings. I'd feel rejected.
- I'd lose the fantasy that the person might have supported me—if I had found the best way to ask.

And let's face it. I was probably afraid that I would fall on my rear end—metaphorically—in front of a top person in the industry.

The Solution to Overcome Career Crippling Mistake #3:

Two things. First, *get effective support.* Second, *rehearse.*

Effective support will help you avoid the "falling-on-one's-rear-end" calamity. When I wanted to ask for an endorsement for my book, I called a friend for support. She helped me craft the email request message. And she remained on the phone while I pressed "send." She acted as my coach, encouraging me through the whole process.

Now, about the second method: I *rehearse* for various important moments in my life. Before I have a first meeting with a client, I make notes and rehearse what I'm going to say—and how I'll respond in a supportive way. Also, when I was preparing for an important radio interview, I rehearsed with two media coaches and three friends.

If I'm going to ask someone for a favor, I get clear on how my favor would be easy for the person to comply with. If possible, I look to see if the favor to me can also benefit my friend. For example, I said to a friend, "I'd like to promote your book from the cover of my book. Would you take a look at my book and see if you feel comfortable in endorsing it?"

Be sure to put effort into being effective at asking. Make sure that the way you ask has three elements: a) it's easy to comply, b) there's something in it for the person, and c) the person is in a good mood to want to help you. As I mentioned earlier, *help them first.*

Remember: Take action and avoid these big mistakes:

1. Putting off networking
2. Failure to make it fun and easy to help you
3. Failure to ask

Success is about doing the right things and avoiding unnecessary mistakes.

Some Thoughts about Networking and Your Personal Brand

Imagine if your personal brand was "someone who helps others all of the time." What if people were delighted to connect you with others? People might say, "Oh, you've got to meet [your name]. . .[he/she] helps people all of the time and knows everybody!"

When coaching my clients and graduate students, I share *a three-word principle about networking: "Help them first."* This is the antidote to any hesitation to asking for help to get a job or accomplish anything else. Why? People are *more receptive* to help us when we help them first.

How do you find out what people need or want? Ask this

question: "How can I be supportive of what you're doing?" This works well because sometimes saying "How can I be supportive of *you*" may be too forward. There's a little emotional distance with "what you're *doing*." Then both you and the other person are looking at activities instead of his or her personal needs.

Now, some of my clients were, at first, hesitant about asking, "How can I be supportive of what you're doing?"

Why? Because they were afraid that someone might ask for too much. Here's an example of how to handle that situation.

Kesha asked her friend, Sandra, a professional speaker, to advertise Kesha's book to Sandra's elist of subscribers—in hopes of gaining sales. Sandra replied, "First, Kesha, I want you to know that I believe in you and your book. Let me check a couple things over here and see if that would be a match. How about I call you tomorrow? I'll likely know more then."

The next day, Sandra called Kesha and said, "I talked this over with my PR tech person. We've noticed that we've recently pushed a number of things to my elist. I don't want to 'burn my list.' I do have some good news. I'm speaking next week to an appropriate group. So I can put your book at my 'autograph' table. I can sell copies of your book at my speaking engagement. How does that sound?"

Kesha was grateful, and Sandra did not cave in to Kesha's first request and hurt herself. Just because someone gives you a request, you do not have to say, "Yes." But when you know what may help the person, you may find that you can be helpful in another way. Help someone first and you're using networking as a way to make friends. Then you can let go of a reluctance to "beg people for leads." You're not begging. Instead you're sharing benefits and kindness. And such sharing inspires people to look on you as trustworthy and worthwhile (an uplifting and effective personal brand).

4) FIND YOUR POWER TO MAKE A TOUGH SPEECH DURING AN ECONOMIC RECESSION

Are you facing a tough speech now—during this economic recession? Will you need to lay off employees? Do you need to shake up your team to change their habits so that your company (or department) can survive and even excel during economic turmoil?

Here are three principles for giving a good speech:

1. I can't persuade you if I don't know you.

If you need to present painful material (like layoffs or the elimination of a department), don't just launch into a cold recitation of facts. First, engage your audience with some "dialogue." That is, ask a few gentle questions and truly listen. People are more receptive if they feel that you're listening to them.

"People don't care how much you know until they know how much you care." — John C. Maxwell

Ask gentle questions. Your asking the questions and listening closely helps make it clear that you care.

Let your audience's answers help you make quick decisions about the order you'll mention your next points and examples.

An important hint for giving a successful speech: Talk with audience members before you give a speech. Then during your speech, you can say something like: "I was talking with a number of you. And Susan mentioned how the XYZ project needed more . . ."

The above comment helps the audience feel: "Yes. She is listening to us. She knows something about what we're going through."

2. We don't need you to be perfect; we need you to be genuine.

Do you think you could give your speech without reading it? It's okay to use 3" X 5" cards. A helpful technique I share with my clients and graduate students is to have a metal ring holding the top left corner of the 3" X 5" cards. If you drop the cards, they remain in the correct order.

My clients and graduate students often tell me how helpful they find my principle "We don't need you to be perfect; we need you to be genuine." They say this principle has helped them speak with more confidence.

One of the first things I teach my graduate students is Recovery Methods. Practicing such methods helps one drop a lot of nervousness. For example, one can say, "Oh, that's not what I meant to say. What I meant to say is ______."

3. It's not real until you tell a story.

If you say something like: "I was talking with Susan Jakque in shipping, and she showed me that . . .," you have the audience's attention. Why? Because you're talking about someone they know and about things that they see on a daily basis. You're not starting with some up-in-the-sky theory. You're starting with a real person and sharing her story.

If you really need to make an important point, tell a well-crafted story. The story gives the audience an experience—that makes it real. You also get to side-step the resistance that naturally arises in audience members. Are all audiences resistant? Good question. Researchers note that people tend to judge any statement. Such judgments may be subconscious. It is almost a reflex to think: "Does that make sense? Do I agree with that?"

For example, I watch faces closely when I give a speech. One day, I said, "Women live longer than men" and I saw one man frown in disagreement. I was on my way to say that it works better to ask a question: "Why do women live longer than men?" — because that engages a different part of an audience members' brain. But even a statement that seem widely accepted, "Women live longer than men," still incites judgments by audience members.

Instead, tell a story about how married men live longer lives, and you have shifted the responses of audience members.

Further, if I say: "I'm a good team member" that doesn't mean much. But if I *tell you a story* of how I walked with a new contractor to another department and helped her get a paycheck in one third the usual time—that action means something.

Now, imagine that you're tasked with informing co-workers that there will be layoffs at the company where you work. A dreadful assignment, I know. Do NOT only tell the bad news. Talk about actual positive stories of how the department's "transition consultant" has helped people find new employment. The stories make the idea of "we'll help you" into something that feels real.

The point is to come across as a truly caring and competent person. To influence someone, you need to make sure that your listener finds you to be Concerned, Competent and Connected. I call these The 3 C's.

Focus your efforts on the three above principles and then your listeners will know:

– that you're concerned about their well-being

– that you're competent to make things work during tough times

– that you are connecting as one human being to another

One final tip: When someone asks you a tough question, make sure you turn your body to face the person. This body language communicates that you're paying full attention. Here's an easy way to remember this body language method. Think "heart faces heart."

Some Thoughts about "Concerned, Competent and Connected" and Your Personal Brand

Earlier in this book, I shared that an effective personal brand demonstrates:

- Who I am
- What you can count on me to do
- What I expect from life

Realize that your habitual ways of talking either build up your personal brand that you're an effective and trustworthy person—or tear you down in the eyes of others. The shortcut is to focus your speech to your audience's preferences to express details related to The 3 Cs: "Concerned, Competent and Connected."

If you demonstrate all three, you prove trustworthy to your listener. If you omit one of the 3 Cs, the person subconsciously puts up their guard.

Here are examples of mistakes that show one does not have The 3 Cs:

- Joe addresses a team member with the wrong name. [Instantly, the person thinks, "You don't give a damn about me. You can't even remember my name!"]
- Karl fumbles as he talks about the new measures that change how the department treats the employees that have not been laid off. [Instantly, the person thinks, "I can't trust you to lead this department. You don't even know what you're talking about!"]
- Jackson delivers bad news about layoffs in the department and does *not* look anyone in the eyes. [Instantly, the remaining people have no confidence that Jackson can get the department out of the hole they're in. The remaining employees cannot trust that Jackson has the personal strength to lead during such difficult times.]

On the other hand, here are examples of demonstrating the 3 Cs—"Concerned, Competent and Connected."

- Deborah addresses Sophie by name and says, "I appreciate how you anticipated Ms. Smith's objection about Project A2. Good work." [Deborah is *connected* emotionally to Sophie.]
- Gladys says, "Today, we're going to streamline the budget for the Kervin job. I recommend that we combine steps G2 and G6. And I'd like to open the discussion for your thoughts and suggestions." [Gladys is *competent* and *concerned* about the team members' point of view.]

Remember, every time you open your mouth, you have an opportunity to demonstrate that you're Concerned, Competent and Connected. Make the most of your opportunity. Build your personal brand and thus your success.

5) HOW CAN YOU GET SOMEONE TO SAY 'YES'?

Ever felt that your life depended on someone saying 'Yes'?

One 'Yes' can change the next five, 10, 25 years of your life.

Don't believe me?

Ever ask, "Will you marry me?"

How about: "Will you publish my book?"

Years ago, I contacted a top agent — I mean top. Within one hour of receiving my book proposal, this agent called me on the phone.

That was promising. I jumped so high that I nearly dented the ceiling with my head.

But . . .

This agent saw my marketing plan (back then) and said, "No."

Do you know why?

One reason was I did not have leverage.

Since that time, I have sold books in 15 countries.

Further, my audio books *Darkest Secrets of Persuasion and Seduction Masters* and *Be Heard and Be Trusted* are available on iTunes.com and emusic.com.

The next time I contact an agent [any agents reading this?], I'm going to bring details like sales in 15 countries and my other marketing accomplishments.

Now . . . listen closely.

The hidden secret to get someone to say 'Yes' to you is . . .

Leverage.

Here's what I mean. Leverage, as I trust you know, is putting little effort in and getting a big result.

Leverage is also power.

Why would someone marry you? Because you have the power to assist that person in having a happy life. [Okay, I know there are other reasons—but let's leave diapers out of this discussion. Oops — too late.]

For business interactions, focus on these *3 Golden Points of Leverage:*

1) your network (your contacts . . . how many people are in your esubscribers list, connected to you via LinkedIn.com, Twitter, Facebook network?)
2) you have special knowledge (you're an expert; perhaps you know current marketing trends)
3) you have access to target markets.

So when you make a presentation in search of the golden "yes," ensure that the person experiences how you have the above *3 Golden Points of Leverage.*

When I talk about giving a person an experience of your leverage, I often refer to Harvey Mackay showing a publisher thousands of Rolodex cards of his contacts. Okay, about the cards, this was some time ago. Harvey achieved his goal: the publisher responded by printing 100,000 copies as a first run.

Here are two more vital parts of getting someone to say "yes" to you:

- help her first
- make it easy and fun to help you

Help Her First

The Law of Reciprocity holds that when you do something for someone, that person feels a pull towards being kind to you in return, to be reciprocal in the interaction. So get a business interaction off to a good start.

Help the other person first. Some big business deals started with the gift of a pen. That may seem odd. But we're talking about getting the other person into a good mood and helping them be receptive to what you're offering.

The idea of a small gift or giving someone a lead to a good prospective client relates to a phrase I often share with audiences: *Small steps can lead to big leaps.*

Make It Easy and Fun to Help You

When is it easy and fun to help someone? First, it's fun because we like helping those people who have been kind to us. Second, some people ask easy, small favors that don't take much time. We're much more inclined to say "yes" to that kind of request.

Avoid asking for too much, too soon. . . . Okay, you could ask but you'd likely burn the bridge before it was fully built and had flame retardant added. Yes, I know, I'm stretching a metaphor . . .

Finally, I want to emphasize, you can only get a "yes," if you ask for the order, that is, you ask for what you want.

You might get a "no" response to your request, but you didn't have what you wanted, anyway. And now, you have more experience in the art of asking. You might even ask, "Obviously, I made a mistake. What would have helped you to say yes to my project?"

Become skillful in gaining leverage and asking—and success will be your constant companion.

Some Thoughts about Leverage and Your Personal Brand

If you want someone to say "Yes" to you, subtly reveal your ability to influence others and get things done. How?

Prepare and tell entertaining stories. A good story begins with a problem that defies solving. The story includes tension, a setback and a miracle save (or rescue). Not every story has all of these elements. But if you take some time and reflect on your favorite personal stories, you'll see these elements. Remember the subtle goal of your story is to demonstrate your leverage—how you have power to influence others and get things done.

And you can take your story up a notch. How? If you want to get people to believe you have a skill or talent, end the story with a comment from a happy client, co-worker or supervisor. You could close a story with something like: "And that's when I completed the project one day ahead of time. And my supervisor Stephanie said, "[your name], I can always count on you to come up with a creative solution to tough problems."

The phrase "a creative solution to tough problems" demonstrates a way to fit in a key part of an effective personal brand. You see closing the story with "count on you" and "to come up with a create solution to tough problems" plants these ideas into the mind of the listener. They form a foundation of an effective personal brand.

In our next section, *Book Four: Expand Your Success*, we'll explore ten methods to help you leap to higher levels of success.

BOOK FOUR:
EXPAND YOUR SUCCESS

If a man is called to be a street sweeper, he should sweep streets even as a Michelangelo painted, or Beethoven composed music or Shakespeare wrote poetry. He should sweep streets so well that all the hosts of heaven and earth will pause to say, "Here lived a great street sweeper who did his job well." — Martin Luther King Jr.

During our dinner gathering, the assembled seven notable people agreed that devoting their whole hearts to their individual focus areas was crucial. They said that in essence they were "all in" when they did their work. Such focus brought about their success.

Imagine that your personal brand includes the perception that *you are successful*. Why would that be important? Because people offer *more opportunities* to those they perceive as successful. They want to work with successful and highly competent people. How do you build that reputation—that personal brand? You work on yourself. Consider yourself to be a "corporate athlete." Get in great shape.

The following 10 topics (which I first introduced in an earlier form on my blog www.BeHeardandBeTrusted.com) will help you develop skills for responding well to tough business events. Developing skills takes effort and that reminds me of author Randy Gage's comment: *"I do what other people won't do so in the future I can do what other people cannot do."*

I invite you to study and practice the following methods covered in the 10 topics below:

1) Unleash Your Power to Succeed through Empowering Questions
2) Your Important Step for Real Success
3) Be True to You and Success Expands
4) Your Best Year Ever—How You Can Welcome Success!
5) Flow to the Next Moment
6) Focus on "I Am Resolved"—And Expand Your Success
7) Take an Important Step for Your Success
8) Focus—Your Power to Succeed
9) Your Success and "Don't Attack the Cat"
10) Drop Limited Thinking and Pump Up Your Success

1) Unleash Your Power to Succeed through Empowering Questions

What would help you the most to increase your income, joy and fulfillment? The answer is actually *using the right questions* to tap into your hidden truth. As a coach, one of the best things that I do is to provide the right questions to help a client find his or her personal answer. Since we're talking about the right questions, we'll use the A.S.K. process:

A – Align
S – Simplify
K – Kindle support

1. Align

Ask yourself: "How am I out of alignment with my personal joy?" Another way to ask this is: "What do I do that interferes with my experiencing some happy moments each day?"

For example, years ago, I worked in a job that was merely for paying the rent. The job had nothing to do with my best skills or my talents. But each day, I aligned myself with gratitude. As I took my morning shower, I told myself, "I'm grateful for the prosperity of this job" and I continued through identifying 10 Blessings. Each morning I felt better about the blessings in my life.

Having an attitude of gratitude can increase your personal energy. The next step is to look to make things better. By asking "How am I out of alignment with my personal joy?" I looked for ways to improve my work life. Things got better.

To this day, I ask myself: "How can I demonstrate to the world, in some way, my talent and how I create valuable results?" Those questions have led to taking appropriate risks. For example, I have written 23 books. For each project, I have hired one to three editors. When I write a book, I'm not certain that the book will gain numerous buyers. But I do know that I will grow as a person while writing the book and being challenged by my editors to improve my writing. To me, writing a book (like this one) and hiring editors is an appropriate risk.

Taking appropriate risks has provided me with many positive adventures including writing, directing and producing feature films.

2. Simplify

An old phrase is: "If anyone says life is not tough, they're either selling you something or delusional." Yes, life can be complicated with all of us facing a lot of obligations and onerous tasks. Even with all of that, here's a vital question: *"What is the Crucial Detail here?"*

By Crucial Detail I mean, what is the most important part of anything you're dealing with. For example, I produced a song for one of my feature films. My friend was a backup singer during the choruses. I wanted him to sound well. Unfortunately, I missed the Crucial Detail: the lead singer was singing too low in her vocal range. I had to scrap the song.

It's really easy to be distracted and to miss the vital element of what you're doing. You can often improve a situation by asking yourself a series of questions, which can lead to your personal Crucial Detail.

Here is an example of such a series of questions:

I asked Joe, a client, this series of questions:

• *What do you want?*

Joe: To write books.

• *What do you get from writing books?*

Joe: A feeling of purpose—to be serving people.

• *How are you feeling on purpose?*

Joe: I like it! I like thinking, exploring, playing with ideas, expressing how I feel and what's important to me—and what life has given me opportunities to learn.

• *How is this important to you?*

Joe: I feel *alive* when writing—and reading the work aloud

to my girlfriend.

When you find something that helps you feel Alive!—then you've uncovered a Crucial Detail. Direct your energy there!

3. Kindle support

Ask yourself: *Who are my Believing Mirrors?* A believing mirror is someone who believes in you and your talent. They know that you can rise to the occasion and express something true and worthy. They show you a "mirror" of how great you can be.

Be careful. Some of the people you really *wish* were a believing mirror (a friend, a family member, a spouse) may NOT be a believing mirror. Then do NOT call them for support. Find people who truly support you. Ask yourself: "Am I just wishing this person would support me? Are they somehow ***incapable*** of being kind and supportive of me? Is it time to find my support *elsewhere*?"

I know someone, "Gertrude," who is a snob about writing. And perhaps she cuts down other writers because she is merely frustrated that she does not finish anything.

Gertrude looks down on any writing that she does not deem "sophisticated." On the other hand, many people acknowledge that there's space in this world for sit-coms, concise prose and literary novels. All writing does not need to be "sophisticated." In any case, I suggest you *avoid people* who provide dream-killing criticism that does not help one improve one's work.

Seek *constructive* feedback. For example, I hire tough editors who push me to make my books better. A good writer and a good athlete welcome "tough but good coaching."

Find your believing mirrors—be kind to them. Bask in their support. Express your appreciation for them. They are true blessings in your life.

Some Thoughts on "Unleash Your Power to Succeed through Empowering Questions"

It's vital to have real support so you have the personal energy to do better and better in your career activities.

What is the most important support you need? Your own support. Treat yourself as you would treat a cherished friend. If you had a good friend stay with you a couple of days, you'd be sure to provide a good place to sleep and blankets, for example. Similarly, you need to provide for your own needs. Along those lines, I provided two questions above to help you identify those needs and related details:

- How am I out of alignment with my personal joy?
- Who are my Believing Mirrors?

Use these questions as springboards to take better care of yourself. This process is vital for your *empowered personal brand.* Make sure that you're seen as someone who is generally upbeat, competent and poised. Why? Because then people can trust you.

Some people say that one can be trustworthy even if one is not upbeat and poised. I submit that a co-worker who is consistently miserable may appear to be too needy and unstable for one to rely on.

When you nurture yourself and improve in the areas of upbeat, competent, poised, and results-oriented, you'll be the last person a manager considers laying off during economic tough times. Also, you'll be the first person offered new opportunities, promotions and raises.

2) YOUR IMPORTANT STEP FOR REAL SUCCESS

I know what to do, but I'm just not doing it," one of my clients lamented. This is a real problem. Often procrastination arises from failing to face difficult truths. For example, I have met a number of people who earned a degree and worked briefly as an attorney. Some of them caused self-sabotage by procrastinating. However, when they finally faced the truth that the daily grind of being an attorney did not suit them, they were able to move forward in life. You can leap to a higher level of success if you learn how to face difficult truths. We'll use the R.E.A.L. process:

R – Reflect
E – Embrace
A – Act
L – Listen

1. Reflect

What's not working in your life? Focus on this question: "What truth must I face?" Take a couple of moments right now with a sheet of paper and note some difficulties. As you write down a problem, focus on your personal truths. Ask yourself: What would I prefer to be different?

I use the word "prefer" with care. Some things are a process. I may prefer that everything happen quickly (right now!) with my project entitled *TimePulse* (to debut as a trilogy of science fiction feature films or a TV series). But it takes time, effort, and restructuring to make something on a high level of excellence.

A number of personal coaches focus on the idea "tolerate

nothing." Their idea is that if you do not like the clutter in your home office, stop tolerating it. Take incremental action to clear things out.

I'll give you an example. It once took me a 30-minute session on 14 days in a row to type up material (and rewrite it as I went along) from a 2-CD set I had recorded. When you reflect and make yourself aware of something that you want to change, settle in to working on it a bit—every day.

2. Embrace

Embrace yourself as a human being with some tendencies you don't like. For example, I simply prefer to write a new book than to do some marketing tasks. I love "making things." And still, I embrace my foibles and hire contractors to do some things. Get someone who is better at some task than you are (perhaps a tax preparer). For example, I have a friend who hired a gardener for $35.00 per month to keep the green areas around his home presentable. This was a good idea because my friend could devote his attention to other areas where his skills and talents were better used.

3. Act

Act. Don't wait to "feel like it." I make a distinction between "want to do" and "feel like it." For example, I often want to complete writing a book—but I may not feel like it. As a professional writer, I have the discipline to sit down and write, regardless of how I'm feeling. I do not wait for inspiration. Inspiration happens while I'm writing.

4. Listen

Once you get a message about what truth you must face, you need to do something unusual: Listen. I'm not saying agree immediately. This is about being coachable. If you won't let any new information in, you cannot improve the situation.

It's amazing sometimes how many friends and family members have advice for us. But here's the truth: You already have the answer you need. Start by asking these empowering questions:

1. What truth must I face?
2. How can I make incremental progress?
3. How can I clear something from my life and create breathing room for myself?

Then answer yourself. Bring your answers to your calendar, PDA, or day planner: Schedule your tasks. Facing the truth is a crucial step for real success and fulfillment.

Some Thoughts on Real Success

Some people I know are embarrassed and will not attend their college reunions. They tell me that they are not successful and have not made a big splash in their career. What is real success? You decide. If you enjoy happy moments each day, that's success. If you help someone breathe a little easier by saying a kind word or offering a bit of help—that's success.

Some of my friends are searching for a new job—but more than that they're exploring new options. At a networking event, someone may ask, "So what do you do?" My friend could say, "I'm currently looking for a position as a sales associate for a company like ___ or ___. And I am finishing up my first novel." Realize that working at a job is just one facet (yes, an important part) of a life. Take an inventory. How many good things are in your life? Do you have friends? Check. Are you kind to people? Check. Are you exploring new career opportunities? Then, part of your success is as "An Explorer." To paraphrase something I heard some years ago, "Success is a way of traveling."

3) BE TRUE TO YOU AND SUCCESS EXPANDS

There's a lot of talk about one's personal brand. Do people know what you stand for? One thing people need to know is that you're reliable. Why? So more people will offer you more opportunities. We'll use the I.N. process:

I – Instill Your Personal Values

N – Nurture Your Best Self

1. Instill Your Personal Values

Do you answer or return phone calls in a short period of time? You never know what opportunities you're losing if people do not trust that you'll get back to them quickly.

I have a wide circle of friends and acquaintances. However, when my company needs contractors, I have a rather short list of people I call. These are people who have demonstrated to me that they are trustworthy and reliable.

When I say "instill your personal values," I mean to make sure people know that you're reliable—that you hold to being respectful. Returning phone calls in a timely manner is respectful. Replying to email messages promptly is also respectful. Keeping promises and commitments is crucial.

Be slow to promise things because it's better not to promise something than to fail to come through.

2. Nurture Your Best Self

Do you have friends who always seem to have plenty of excuses? It's likely that they do not realize the damage they're causing to their prospects for more success. How? Often, people ask for referrals. Each time you or I recommend someone, we're sticking our neck out. It's natural, then, that we will not recommend someone who fails to be on time for social events (for example).

One way to make sure that you take action as your best self is to have a personal code of conduct. Angelina Jolie had tears in her eyes when she talked about her deceased mother's motto: "Be brave, be true, be bold, be kind, be you."

When you are true to yourself, you create a tendency to be true to other human beings.

One of my favorite quotes is:

If you want other people to be happy, practice compassion.
If you want to be happy, practice compassion.
– The Dalai Lama

But our compassion isn't reserved just for others. We're also invited to practice compassion toward ourselves. What does that mean? For many, it can include taking a hard look at your own schedule. Are you overcommitted? Do you need to devote more time to rest and recovery? I know personally that I bring better energy to situations when I'm rested and have good nutrition and exercise.

Take care of yourself, and you can take care of others in your life, too.

Some Thoughts on "Be brave, be true, be bold, be kind, be you" and Success

Someone may be successful in making money and be miserable as a person. Throughout this book, I'm emphasizing an integrated view of one's personal brand. It's not just about sales or money, it's about how you travel in life. Do people smile when you enter a room? At any given moment, something is going in a way we do *not* prefer. Kids are misbehaving. A lover is overwhelmed with work, and you feel lonely. But when you focus on your life with a "Be brave, be true, be bold, be kind, be you" attitude, you realize that there are significant parts of your life that you can and do influence.

For example, you can speak your truth (carefully when appropriate). For example, one of my friends was trying to control me; she kept telling me what stories not to say and what quotes not to repeat. So I decided to avoid attending a gathering she was hosting because I wanted to relax that particular weekend. As a public speaker and graduate school instructor, I must be on my toes. But my discretionary time belongs to me. So I decided to be bold, be true to myself, and be kind to myself.

Look into your own daily patterns. Where can you choose to be true to yourself and to be kind to yourself? Find those points, and you'll recover your personal calm and poise. That will help your personal brand. With more calm and poise, you'll attract more opportunities.

4) YOUR BEST YEAR EVER—HOW YOU CAN WELCOME SUCCESS!

Let's begin this discussion with the thought that today (no matter what day of this year it is) and stepping forward from this moment is what counts. You can brighten each day; take action to make this year into your terrific year. We'll use the A.L.L. process:

A – Align with your heartfelt desires
L – Lift up
L – Learn

1. Align with your heartfelt desires

Are you doing something related to your dreams each day? One year when I was not making much space for writing, I wrote: "Writers write or they're not writers, right?" Simplistic, perhaps. But it served like a boot in the rear to get me writing. Now, I tend to write every day.

What do you really want—from your heart?

I like making films, so I'm sure that I'll be making a couple of films this year.

Identify something that you can do on a modest level that can lead to more opportunities. A number of singers record themselves doing covers of popular songs, and they place videos on YouTube.com. I have bought a number of songs from iTunes.com after discovering less well-known artists' work.

And it is legendary that Usher saw Justin Bieber's cover versions of his songs. Usher became Justin's song producer. So Justin went from YouTube.com to superstardom.

2. Lift up

Lift up your eyes to possibilities. There's always that first time. The first time you sell a book you've written. The first time you actually glide on the dance floor after eight sessions of ballroom dance lessons.

You need to lift up your own eyes. It is likely that you know a number of people who don't have the hope or imagination that something great can happen. Don't let their downer energy hold you back.

Realize that before anyone makes a big leap forward, they need to hold the idea in their mind.

Recently, I saw a documentary about the six films of the *Rocky* franchise. It all began with one man and one dream. Sylvester Stallone wanted to play leading roles in film. He invested his energy and efforts in writing *Rocky* in long-hand on a pad of paper. His then-wife typed up the screenplay.

You cannot win if you don't get in the game. *Rocky* was not Stallone's first screenplay. In fact, the producers who ultimately produced *Rocky* saw Stallone's other written work and said, "What else have you got?"

Lift up your eyes and hope—and get busy. (I invite you to see the free chapter of my book *Nothing Can Stop You This Year!: How to Unleash Your Hidden Power to Persuade Well, Get More Done, Gain Sudden Profits, Command Intuition and Feel Great* at Amazon.com.)

3. Learn

Each time you try something new, you win if you learn something . . . even if things turn out in some disappointing way.

Friends often try to protect you from disappointment. They may say, "Do you know how hard it is to do that?" Or "Do you know how unlikely it is that you'll succeed at that? At getting a big audience?"

Recently, I met with a new colleague. He asked, "How much money can be made with that project?"

I truthfully replied, "It could make no money at all. You need to discover if you really want to do this."

Some projects lead to bigger and better. For example, the TV series *Sanctuary* began as an eight-webisode series that was released via the Internet in 2007. In 2008, the Syfy Channel released the *Sanctuary* TV series. *Sanctuary* has continued with the current 4th season.

As I mentioned, if you learn something, you always win. I've learned to be really good about setting budgets for projects. Why? Because I want the freedom to explore and to experiment. So I have multiple projects going at any time—and any one of them can become "red hot." That's when I focus more resources on that particular project.

To keep my focus, I have a written list of goals, and I've learned to postpone some projects. For example, I have already written down two projects that I'm postponing to next year.

So make this year (or this month) one of joy, stretching to fulfill your potential, and personal fulfillment.

Remember to:

A – Align with your heartfelt desires

L – Lift up

L – Learn

Some Thoughts on "What do you really want—from your heart?" and Success

What we really want is often about what we want to feel. Why would you want to have a significant other or be married? Probably because you want to feel warm, nurtured—and to have a chance to give your love to another person. I've noticed that some of my most joyful times have involved *my being kind* to my sweetheart. It wasn't about something she did for me; it was about how I felt acting in a loving, compassionate way. I had the *chance to be the best I could be.*

When what you do for your living involves—at least in part—being at your best, you'll simply feel better. And then you will do better. So the pattern is: do something that expresses your best, feel better, do better—and get offered more opportunities. For example, many years ago, I did my best while working in the tech department of a bank. I was an operations analyst. But what I really did was help people get solutions and then feel better. I did this well, and a vice president helped me get other opportunities. My personal brand was competent, friendly, and helpful. That was an effective personal brand. See how you can enhance your own personal brand.

5) FLOW TO THE NEXT MOMENT

Have you ever wanted to really feel joy? Successful people I have interviewed squeeze each day like an orange and get the juice. How? They bounce back quickly after tough moments. They find the discipline to "flow to the next moment." We'll use the Y.E.S. process:

Y – Yield the judgments
E – Embrace possibilities
S – Savor

1. Yield the Judgments

"I'm sorry that you're having a bad day," a friend may say. Really? The whole day is bad? That is a false judgment if you buy into it, and it causes trouble because it limits your perception.

For example, recently I had a choice in a personal situation. A member of my extended family unloaded a lot of judgmental comments on me. It felt so burdensome that I replied, "That's being judgmental." Finally, after being pummeled by the person's rant, I said, "Judge this. I cancel." With that, I cancelled my participation in a get-together.

During the previous week I had demonstrated great patience with the same unruly person, but at that moment when I said "I cancel," I was missing two important things: "reserves" and "capacity." I admit it: I was exhausted after completing final grades for 7 classes of graduate students and college students.

Now here is where the big choice comes in. Do I interpret this unpleasant exchange (my family member's ranting) as making a whole day bad? Or do I choose to say, I just went through some bumpy moments, and let's see what's next? This relates to my phrase "flow to the next moment."

So when I say "yield the judgments," I mean "give up your judgments." Why? They won't serve you, anyway. If I judge a day ruined by some "bumpy moments," then I simply hurt myself. Further, I disrupt the day of the people near me with my continued bad mood. On the other hand, when I focus on "flow to the next moment," I free up new energy and new possibilities.

2. Embrace possibilities

Have you ever heard someone say something that is so bitter and so "frozen in the past"? Perhaps, your neighbor "George" says something like: "You know how my father is. It'll be another uncomfortable moment when he criticizes Janet's weight."

Does George know for sure what his father will say in this next moment? No. And even if his father does say something critical, perhaps Janet and the other people present will be feeling so good that the critical remark just "bounces off."

To have the chance to embrace possibilities, we need to choose to let go of our predictions.

3. Savor

It helps to step into each moment fresh and to enjoy what you find in that particular moment. This is especially relevant during the holiday season. We remember the good times and want them to happen again. But that's not possible. The people around you are not the same. You're not the same. So, instead, imagine that the next moment will be "good and different."

Let this next moment be what it is. Savor whatever you find that is positive in this present moment.

Shake off the dust of the past, and flow to the next moment. That's where we do our real living! In each moment, we have the possibility to discover joy, surprise, love, compassion, and connection.

Many joyful moments.

Some Thoughts on "Yield the Judgments" and Success

"What an a**!" I've heard a number of times from colleagues as they expressed frustration about a client, co-worker or supervisor. I understand that people do feel frustration. However, I suggest that they *quickly reframe the judgmental thought* to something like: "Okay. I'm frustrated with Joe's failure to get me the document. Maybe he's having a bad day."

Why is this reframing useful? Imagine what your face and your body language do when you're judging someone else to be a substandard human being. Disdain leaks out through your eyes and voice. Your body leans away from the other person. Humans pick up these subtle cues. You may be on your way to making an enemy.

So I invite you to avoid staying in "judgmental mode" when looking at other people. And *especially avoid spilling your judgments* about other people to your co-workers. You don't want to get a reputation as a bitter, judgmental person. That will torpedo your personal brand. If you need to vent, then vent to a piece of paper and rip it up (so no one will see it—I call this the *Write Down, Rip Up Method*). Or hire a personal coach or therapist.

Do *not* let being a judger/complainer act as your predominant mode of interacting with the world. Sure, you can observe repeated behaviors and deem them not helpful. And you can act accordingly—such as avoiding being at the mercy of a procrastinator. Still, be sure to bring some compassion to your view of other people. Your positive energy will enhance your personal brand.

6) FOCUS ON "I AM RESOLVED"—AND EXPAND YOUR SUCCESS

Do you have just a vague idea about how you'd like your life to improve? No one got energized by vague, wishy-washy goals. Your real power ignites when you say, "I am resolved." We'll use the A.M. process:

A – Aim high

M – Make it a game you can win

1. Aim high

Yes—have a big goal. Why? No one got excited by "Yeah, join us. We're making something mediocre."

So when I begin a project, I'm not thinking just one book. I'm thinking "Trilogy!"

No. More than that. I'm thinking books, graphic novels, and feature films—and a TV series.

Someone may ask me, "Have you done a TV series?"

I reply, "Not yet."

"Have you met Steven Spielberg?"

"Not yet."

Someone else may ask, "How do you even think you'd meet Steven Spielberg?"

I reply, "Have your heard of my book *TimePulse: Beyond Titanic*? One of his team members may bring it to his attention. Spielberg might get interested in that." [If you're curious, see the first 9 chapters at Amazon.com.]

To jump forward, you need to take good steps. You need to be in the game to have a chance to win it.

2. Make it a game you can win

I know a filmmaker who had a film that didn't make any money. An absolute failure—yes?

She told me, "We had three goals:

- Make something that uplifted people
- Further our careers
- Make money.

We got two out of three."

Many people would say that two out of three is not an absolute failure. And certainly, she is now motivated to do projects "that make money." And she learned so much with her first film.

So . . . how can you "make it a game you can win"?

First, identify goals that you have real control over. What are those? I call them Effort-goals. You control how many pages you write a day. You control how many agents you submit a query letter to. Here we're talking about "I am resolved." So with an Effort-goal, you can say something like: "I am resolved to write my book this year. I am resolved to write at least 100 words each day."

It's reported that the first *Chicken Soup for the Soul* book was rejected 130 times. How many of us would have given up at 99 submissions to publishers?

So target your Effort-goals. Give yourself a reward for accomplishing each of your Effort-goals.

The other form of a goal is a Result-goal like this: "I am resolved to have an agent accept my book and represent me." Do you control that? Not really. But you do control how many query letters or email messages that you send. You control whether you place yourself in a position where good fortune can occur.

One of my mentors told me, "Have three screenplays at all times. One screenplay out there in the marketplace; one screenplay that you're finishing; and one screenplay that you're starting." Why? Because if no one buys the "script that is out in the marketplace," you are okay because you've already moved onward with a new script.

Give yourself credit for making daily steps with your Effort-goals. Make it a game you can win.

Focus on what you really want and discover the power when you say to yourself, "I am resolved to . . ."

– write three pages today

– make fifteen marketing phone calls

– send two query letters

– take a 45-minute walk with my spouse and talk about our day

Be resolved to take action for what is most important for your life and happiness.

Some Thoughts on "I Am Resolved" and Success

"A goal is a wish with a deadline." I wish I had written that comment.

But when it comes to writing, I do not live in "wishes."

I live in "I am resolved."

For example, I wrote a book in 70 days once. I had four editors working on it simultaneously (each editor worked on a separate section). Simultaneously, I taught 125 graduate students and college students. I wrote every day.

Why did I write so fast? Well, one reason was because the topic was painful to me. It related to the suicide of one of my close friends. I felt like I needed to "do something."

I really take to heart the comment:

"The only thing necessary for the triumph of evil is for good men to do nothing." – Edmund Burke

So I did something with my team of editors. I wrote a book. If you'd like to see two free chapters on Amazon.com, the title is *Darkest Secrets of Spiritual Seduction Masters: How to Protect Yourself, Boost Your Psychological Immune System and Strengthen Your Spirit.*

Get yourself to the place of "I am resolved."

I'm glad that I endured the 70 days of writing that book.

And I'm grateful for the team who sustained me through the journey.

To be successful, you'll need to push yourself farther than you ever thought you could go. Choose loving and competent people to sustain you.

7) TAKE AN IMPORTANT STEP FOR YOUR SUCCESS

What do you really want? How can you get from where you are to where you truly want to be? Take a step each day. Use my phrase "Better than Zero." We'll use the U.P. process:

U – Use spare moments

P – Pick an easy part

1. Use spare moments

Some of my best ideas arrive as I rest on a train on my way to San Francisco to teach graduate students. I'm not straining or fretting in front of a blank computer screen. As soon as an idea arrives, I write it down.

At this moment, I feel grateful to my team members who helped me this year with their editing of 7 books I wrote and published. How did I manage to write so many books? I wrote every day. Some days, I only wrote 100 words, but all of those words added up. Use your spare moments to take small steps toward your goals.

As I mentioned earlier, one book took 70 days, while I had four editors working on different parts of the book simultaneously. Yes, I teach 7 classes to graduate students and college students . . . and I use spare moments to make my dreams happen.

2. Pick an Easy Part

Pick some part of the project that is easy for you to do. I call this the Easy Part Start. Writing a book? Start with chapter titles. Or better yet—write the "fun section to write" first! You'll gain momentum. Every day I write down how many words I've written. The principle I use is: Keep score and achieve more. Another principle is: Make it a game you can win. When I tell myself that writing something, even just 10 words, is a "win," then I have no hesitation. Writing 10 words is "Better than Zero."

I invite you to discover the power of "Better Than Zero."

I have heard a number of people say things like "I can't attend the whole-day workshop." How about attending 2/3 of the day? It's Better than Zero.

Another person says, "I can't get the perfect gift." How about getting a small gift? Again, Better than Zero.

Author Alan Weiss wrote: "You're searching for perfection not success." He implies that success often involves making progress and not waiting for the elusive "perfect time."

Improve your own life. Take a step forward each day. A step. Not a "perfect step."

As a side note: Another Alan Weiss comment is "Real wealth is discretionary time. Money is merely fuel for that wealth."

I include this comment because life is about joy, love, compassion, fulfillment, courage, humility, and trustworthiness (and more). Some people seem to hold out for the "perfect job that brings in a lot of money." How about a job that takes care of expenses and expands your capabilities—and allows you to have a life outside of work?

Remember, *Better than Zero.*

Make today a better day, and your tomorrow will blossom as well.

Some Thoughts on "Better Than Zero" and Success

To be successful, focus on putting one foot in front of the other. That works for climbing Mt. Everest, and it works for losing weight (I prefer to say "getting lighter")—or maintaining physical fitness. In fact, since this topic has come up, I'm going to step outside for my daily run now.

I'm back from a brief run. How long? 10 minutes for today. Later, I'll do sit-ups, kicks, palm strikes (martial arts), pushups, and more. But at the moment, I'm under significant writing deadlines.

Remember "Better than zero." If you injure your foot, you can do "chair aerobics" (there are videos about that available at Amazon.com and elsewhere). Years ago, I noticed that my strength improved and my feelings of well being were enhanced with merely 10 pushups a day (I do more exercises now). Of course, when it comes to exercise, we're all advised to check in with our doctor first.

My point is: Success is often about incremental improvements and developing wholesome habits.

Better than zero.

8) FOCUS—YOUR POWER TO SUCCEED

Some people seem to be a "wandering generality," and they're complaining about feeling stuck. It's understandable. Why? Because a human being needs to focus, and focusing gets you out of the "stuck place." What we need to do is ask more of ourselves and ask more of life. So we'll use the A.S.K. process:

A – Ask tough questions
S – See with new eyes
K – Keep experimenting

1. Ask tough questions.

Here are some tough questions:

- Why are you here?
- What makes you happy?
- How does your life have meaning?

For more than eleven years, I have had an unwavering Personal Mission: "I help people experience enthusiasm, love and wisdom to fulfill big dreams." Yes, I've memorized it.

It's comforting to know my focus. It makes it easier to make good decisions.

Here's another good question: Why are you doing what you're doing?

You've probably heard of a company Mission Statement.

Mission Statements work well when they're reduced to a couple of lines:

We create energizing, empowering edutainment for our good and humankind's rise.

– Mission Statement of Tom Marcoux Media, LLC

Yes, I've memorized this statement, too.

To see our projects, you could visit our "Tom Marcoux Media LLC" Facebook page or visit my website TomSuperCoach.com (or visit my blog at BeHeardandBeTrusted.com).

So what's your Mission Statement? Don't hesitate. Write a rough draft now.

2. See with new eyes.

"It's not that *life* is boring. *You* are boring," said author Anthony Robbins. Someone who finds life to be boring is "seeing with old eyes." On the other hand, to see with new eyes is to be a "good finder" and to be "an experimenter." One year, I told friends, "I'm trying an experiment. I'm going to run 10 minutes a day for 30 days." I even confided, "I don't even know if I like running." So when I did that 30 day experiment, I saw new sights and felt new things, too. What about you? What can you try that's new—that you have some interest in?

3. Keep experimenting.

In reading 85 books during one year, I see over and over that people who have big successes try a number of projects. The company that hit the jackpot with the Thighmaster (earning over $100 million) had eight projects in their initial plan. Thighmaster was number two.

Currently, I have 23 books available online (free chapters available at Amazon.com).

Some of the books gain more readers than others. And this is okay because we all have different tastes.

Over the years, I keep learning, exploring and experimenting.

Tom J. Watson, a pro golfer, said, "If you want to increase your success rate, double your failure rate." In other words, if you want to eventually succeed, keep trying, keep making those attempts.

This is a helpful idea that needs an added idea: "Design your projects and marketing plans so that you 'don't lose the store.'" My point is to take risks but also have ways to be okay if things take an unfortunate turn.

About experimenting . . . Recently, I called a friend to share a high-five moment; I felt good about completing a rather large writing project.

He looked at a sample of 1500 words and obsessed over one verb. One verb! As if that one verb would cause over 80,900 words of material to crash and burn.

How about that? He became just another "harsh reviewer." Harsh reviewers have some ideal picture of what a project "should be." They parade their opinions as "facts."

On the other hand, as an artist, I have opportunities to finish things and enhance my skills while I'm expressing my gifts. Do you know what I did with my friend's rejection of my work? I "celebrated that someone disagrees." That means, I celebrated my courage to put my work into the world. A different friend said, "If you haven't earned someone's anger, you have not made an impact."

I invite you to experiment and to be an artist. Let the "reviewers" amuse themselves.

This section is about your choosing to focus.

Let's return to the tough questions that can help you focus on the important parts of your life:

- Why are you here?
- What makes you happy?
- How does your life have meaning?
- Why are you doing what you're doing?

Write down your rough draft answers now. And you're on your way!

Some Thoughts on "Celebrate that Someone Disagrees" and Success

What do you do when someone criticizes your work? Do you slink away and cast the unworthy work aside? Or do you look for a kernel of truth that you might use to improve the work? In any case, consider developing your own patterns to "Celebrate that Someone Disagrees." This is important because no matter what, you must be your own best cheerleader.

Every work is likely to have at least a couple of fans and plenty of detractors. Why? Because everyone has personal preferences. Some people avoid horror films. I see few horror films, but one of my top favorite films is *Jaws*, directed by Stephen Spielberg. There is no telling what the marketplace will be like when you bring a work to it. Some films like *The Princess Bride* are late bloomers, finding their audience on VHS, then DVD, and now on Blu-ray.

Prepare for the times when someone dislikes your work. Tell your friends and family about your "Celebrate that Someone Disagrees." Usually, in my home, my sweetheart and I go out, and she gets chocolate, and I get a new book (less filling and no calories!).

If you're doing something original and valuable, someone is bound to disagree. That's okay; that's their right. And you have the right to pick up your own morale and "Celebrate that Someone Disagrees." Keep practicing "your art"—whether it's writing or just having a kind word for co-workers or friends. You'll get better at it. And that is truly successful.

9) YOUR SUCCESS AND "DON'T ATTACK THE CAT"

Do you want more harmony in your life? Would you like your journey of success to flow more smoothly? Then "Don't attack the cat." Say what?

I was inspired to create this phrase by an episode of the Animal Planet show entitled *My Cat from Hell.* If a guy plays rough with a cat, the cat will lie in wait for any person in the house and then pounce and take a swing with his claw. The idea is to think through the possible consequences before you take action. We'll use the C.A.T. process:

C – Consider restraint

A – Act to encourage peace

T – Transform

1. Consider restraint

I've seen a number of guys who like to "play rough with the cat." Is that how the cat sees it? As playing? These guys laugh and say, "It's fun."

Oh yeah? Having a cat as a guerilla warrior in your house is fun? You see, you have inadvertently trained a cat to "play" by attacking you in return. Not a good idea.

People can be similar to a cat. If you say things that put someone on the defensive, that person may always be on edge when you're around. Not only that, but some people may also become resentful and look for ways to get back at you.

My main point is: Don't fall into bad habits. Instead, pause. Think it through. And consider what pattern you may be setting up. In sum, "Don't attack the cat."

2. Act to encourage peace

I recall a song with the lyrics, "Let there be peace on earth. And let it begin with me."

I encourage you to think through the consequences before you say something casually. I've noticed that some people like to "tease." The problem is that people may find that the humor is biting and they may develop resentment toward the one doing the teasing. Avoid the whole problem: let peace begin with you by saying encouraging things.

You can say:

- "That was a good job you did on wrapping that gift."
- "Section 3A was a well-written part of the report. Thanks for your effort on that."
- "You know what I like about you? You always find something kind to say."

3. Transform

Transformation occurs in this present moment. Learning takes time. But transformation can be instantaneous.

Imagine that it is not about learning something, but about clearing space to be present, here and now, and to let things be as they are. The opposite of "letting things be" is resistance. Resistance puts you at a distance from people and life.

Transform the nature of your relationships. Pause. Look for encouraging things to say. Be sure to listen and hear the other person out. Avoid any casual comments that might feel like an attack to the person you're talking with.

And remember, to create peace and harmony . . . "Don't attack the cat."

Do express your appreciation.

For example, my cat tends to seek me out at 1:07 AM every morning for his "cat rub down." (He's taught me how to scratch behind his ears just right. Then he lifts his chin, saying "You missed a spot.")

Here's a cat who feels comfortable.

Let's set each other at ease.

Some Thoughts on Resistance and Success

Some time ago, I came up with the idea for a book called *Darkest Secrets of Persuasion and Seduction Masters.* It began with how I was angry about some manipulative techniques that were used on a couple of friends. I sat down and wrote 2,000 words in one hour. But then I hesitated. I was concerned that the title of such a book was "too sensationalistic." I felt resistance.

Since that time, I have written a total of 9 books in the *Darkest Secrets . . . How to Protect Yourself* series. I gave up my resistance and found that there was a large audience for this series of books. I always remember this quote:

"We must be willing to relinquish the life we planned, so as to have the life that is waiting for us." — Joseph Campbell.

I now embrace that I have become more than America's Communication Coach. I've become a "Strength and Self-Protection" Coach, too. I now say: "It's good to strengthen yourself to empower your dreams." In learning my life lessons over the years, I've learned to strengthen myself, my resolve, and my ability to adapt and go around obstacles. Now, I do that for readers like you and for my clients and audiences.

Success often arrives when we learn to let go of knee-jerk resistance. Open your eyes to what delightful surprise opportunities life has for you. That is a path of success *and* fulfillment. Enjoy.

10) DROP LIMITED THINKING AND PUMP UP YOUR SUCCESS

When you're right you know it–yes? Are you sure? Have you ever been so certain about something and then later you discovered your perception was off? Let's focus on what is going on below the surface. Why do we tend to make other people wrong? To get the "prize" of certainty. It's almost as if our subconscious mind is ringing with: "You're wrong, so I'm right. Good. Now, I can feel safe." To improve our business and personal relationship, we'll use the H.O.W. process:

H - Honor
O - Own
W - Welcome

1. Honor

I'm using the word "honor" as a verb. Honor that both you and the other person can be right (in some manner) at the same time, even though you disagree.

Let's say that Susan and Mark are arguing. She says, "Stop yelling at me." And he responds, "I'm not yelling." They can both be right. He may be talking at a "medium" level compared to the household discussions he grew up with. And she may be hearing his tone as "harsh." In her family, the big taboo was raising one's voice. Only later in a couple's therapy session, Susan and Mark can give each other some leeway. Mark says, "I'm sorry that my tone was intense." And Susan can say, "I realize that I might be extra sensitive to how loud somebody talks."

2. Own

Become aware of your own uncertainty. Let's face it. Uncertainty hurts, or at least feels terribly uncomfortable. So what do we do? We just refuse to "sit with the uncertainty," which means to just pause and feel the feelings. Instead, we may subconsciously jump to a conclusion: "Someone must be to blame here. And it can't be me."

Instead, try something different. Pause. When? Whenever you feel the discomfort of uncertainty. For example, I remember being in a coaching session with my own coach. She suggested an idea about how I could deal with a bitter friend, and I paused. A moment later, I replied, "I don't know how to do that yet." The idea was for me to just take a look at a new possibility.

Over the years, I have heard people say, "I don't see how that would help" in response to any new idea that may push them out of their comfort zone. An innovative solution to a problem is likely to stir things up and cause some discomfort. Just because we can't see the value of something at this moment, it does NOT mean that the other person is wrong. Perhaps we just haven't arrived at the point where we can let in a new idea or to get on the same page with the other person.

On the other hand, I have trained myself to avoid dismissing a new idea simply because I feel some discomfort. When leading a team producing a film or book, I often say, "I'll ponder that" to a team member offering a new idea. This is my method to avoid instantly dismissing someone's new idea. It's also my way to own my personal uncertainty. Team members have told me that they appreciate that I do NOT "shut them down." They appreciate that I will hear them out.

3. Welcome

Learn to welcome the surprises of life. Two things can happen: 1) you'll adapt or 2) you'll be pleasantly surprised and delighted. And welcome that other people have varying viewpoints on any given topic.

Each of my 23 books available on Amazon.com (all of them posted with free chapters) was much improved because I welcomed the input and guidance of two editors per book.

The top successful people I know welcome coaching and constructive feedback. Listening to feedback can be tough. After working with the editing comments for a section of a book that I'm writing, I can feel worn out. But I know that my openness to making improvements truly serves my readers. So I endure receiving tough, constructive comments.

Here's an important point: *You cannot grow and improve if you make an impenetrable barrier between you and new ideas and other viewpoints.*

Instead, make yourself stronger and improve your performance at various tasks, when you don't default to making someone else wrong. Focus on Honor, Own, and Welcome.

Some Thoughts on "Honor, Own, Welcome"—and Success

Your personal brand is a promise of performance. Do you promise to honor other people?

If you did honor people, many of them would feel good feelings toward you. Have you ever gone into a store and met a positive salesperson who made you feel welcome? Didn't that brighten your day? You can be a similar-extraordinary person. How? Just before you interact with someone ask yourself, "How can I honor them?"

Above I shared: "Become aware of your own uncertainty." Let's face it: uncertainty feels deeply uncomfortable. Many of us will run from uncertainty and leap at the chance to blame someone else for our bad feelings. I know people who repeatedly say things like: "Your brother made me mad" and "That salesman's a jerk and he ruined my whole day." Improvement of relations requires that we *own* our part of the situation. People who indulge in constantly blaming others have created their personal "victim mentality."

I know what that looks like. When I was nine years old, I studied judo. The teachers would hit the students with plastic bats if we failed to run in place with our knees rising to our chests. I hated getting hit. But I said nothing to my parents; I did not even say, "I want to quit the judo class." I just endured the situation. I just assumed that was the way things were. At nine-years-old, in that judo class, I had a victim mentality.

When I became an adult, I developed a *leadership mentality*. If something is off, I *speak up*. For example, years ago, three of my friends once wanted to corner me about how they wanted me to change and give me a "talking to." Instead of just taking it, I said, "I'm interested in talking with each of you separately. I'm interested in learning new things. For example, I work with a personal coach. But, considering my history of physically defending myself from multiple attackers, the three-on-one plan does *not* work for me." So I informed them that if they surprised me at some gathering, I would simply leave the room. I refused to be cornered by three aggressive people. And I did talk with each friend separately. It turned out that there was a misunderstanding.

So honor yourself. Take care of yourself like a cherished friend. Second, own your personal feelings. Develop a leadership mentality, and this action can expand your success.

Next, we'll explore *Book Five: Your Personal Brand and Your Reputation (Experience Happiness).* You'll learn 10 methods to enhance your happiness. And then people will feel more comfortable in your presence. You'll radiate positive energy.

BOOK FIVE: YOUR PERSONAL BRAND AND YOUR REPUTATION (EXPERIENCE HAPPINESS)

The premise of this book is that improving your personal brand is crucial for you to save time, reduce stress and make more money. Your personal brand is useful for more than job interviews and marketing. Actually your personal brand is *your empowered mode for all business communication.* The way you communicate determines, in a large part, how your career blossoms. Here is a crucial secret: More opportunities arrive for business people who have a pleasant demeanor. Why? Because people, in essence, run from those who are tough to be around.

Imagine if your personal brand included: "a person who is generally happy." Why would that be important? Because people feel comfortable around those who are generally happy.

In our dinner gathering, Albert Einstein said, *"There are*

only two ways to live your life. One is as though nothing is a miracle. The other is as though everything is a miracle."

Those assembled agreed that living as if everything is a miracle is a process that brings more happiness.

One of my friends, "Janet," told me, "I'm not happy, but I'm cheerful." And I thought how sad. And through the years, Janet has said things like, "My life is like I'm Indiana Jones running in front of the large rolling boulder." Would you like to talk to this person?

The one whose life reeks with havoc? Who thinks she can trip and get smashed at any moment?

Janet is living on the edge. She does not have the capacity and *the reserves of energy and emotional strength* so that she can welcome new opportunities into her life. Her constant complaining and "woe is me" talk forms a personal brand of weakness and gloom. But that is NOT for you.

Along the lines of having a reserve, Author Thomas J. Leonard wrote: "When you have enough time and resources to respond to opportunities that are always waiting in the wings, you have a *superreserve*."

People who experience happiness have a reserve (or Leonard's term *superreserve*) of positive energy. To create more success in your life, realize that you need to provide yourself with nourishment: physical, emotional and spiritual.

Let's build up your emotional reserves. Now, we'll cover 10 topics to help you develop more happiness and reserves in your life.

1) Find Your Hidden Power to Bounce Back
2) Make the Most of Your Life
3) Reward Yourself with a Special Gift

4) How You Can Recharge and Make Big Things Happen in Your Life
5) What Four Words Will Make You Stronger?
6) Talk About What You Love
7) Open the Door so You Feel Happy
8) Watch Out for 3 Words that Can Get You In Trouble
9) Protect Your Time and Find New Energy
10) Free Up Your Energy and Get More Done

1) Find Your Hidden Power to Bounce Back

If someone said something vicious, do you have a quick way to guard your own energy and morale? We'll use the I.T. process to take care of ourselves:

I – Inquire
T – Target your transition

1. Inquire

Let's start with a question: "What's your transition?" By transition, I'm talking about your personal way to move out of a bad mood into an empowered mood. Successful people have flexibility. They don't let one thing create a "bad day." Why? Because they want to get a lot accomplished today! A bad mood slows people down.

So what are our tools to get back to an empowered mood? Thoughts and movement.

When Dr. Fred Luskin and I were both guest experts on a television show, he mentioned, "Forgiveness is ending a cycle of blame and suffering." Now that's an important thought.

I have taken this idea to heart and it came in handy just a couple of days ago. The elderly relative of someone I know said something vicious to me.

I implemented a plan to stop the suffering:

1) I stepped away from the rigid, inconsiderate person.

2) I thought through the situation and considered these questions:

– What can I learn here?

– Would this person be rude to anyone else in a similar situation? (Ahh! There's an insight. It's time to not take this personally.)

– Does this person care at all about my view? (No. So it's better to place my time and efforts elsewhere.)

The above process focuses on thought. Now, let's look at movement: I drove some distance away from the bitter person's home and took a walk. Afterward, I felt refreshed, which meant I could go on with my day, ensuring my own productivity.

2. Target your transition

When I say "target," I mean aim for getting yourself back to an empowered mood. An important element of "targeting" is your personal preparation. Think through what steps you personally need to take to get to a better mood.

Remember movement. Perhaps taking a walk would help.

Some people go to a room, close the door, blast some music and dance or do some other form of exercise.

Two things are going on here. First, we're talking about

salvaging the rest of your day — so a bad mood does not cripple you and your productivity.

Second, it's time to assess if some unhealthy patterns of relating exist and whether professional help is appropriate. If someone abuses you, get away and get help.

However, I'm really talking here about the smaller everyday upsets when people's personalities bump against each other.

Learning to guard your own personal energy is vital to your career success and general well being. You don't have the "luxury" to fall into so-called "normal behavior patterns." Many people I have met do not seem to have big goals and the desire to squeeze each day like an orange–to get the juice. Those individuals are okay with holding grudges and saying, "Then she said ___. It ruined my whole day."

But that is NOT for you. You'll take control of your day. How? You'll learn to focus on developing your own personal ways to make a transition from a bad mood to an empowered mood. It's worth it: Your life can be so much better for it!

Some Thoughts about "Find Your Hidden Power to Bounce Back" and Your Personal Brand

When you become an expert at using your own personal "transitions," you'll enjoy more positive personal energy than other people who don't take conscious control of their own emotional life. Another benefit is: You'll put other people at ease. How? You'll radiate positive energy, and you'll have a pleasant demeanor. Your clients (or co-workers) will feel comfortable around you. If you own your own company, you'll find that people enjoy referring new business to you. Develop your own list of transitions you can make before you interact with your supervisor or clients. Write down items like: "Take a walk. Step away and listen to music during a break." Remember, we're talking about your personal brand as your empowered mode for *all* business communication. When we look at communication, we must realize that body language speaks louder than words. Why? Because every person's subconscious mind is scanning for messages delivered by posture and gestures. We even have mirror neurons (brain cells) that are attuned to the moods and subtle messages of others.

So it is a *business necessity* to learn to transition from a bad mood to an empowered mood. You can watch your words. But a better state of being will be the crucial ingredient for placing others at ease in your presence. And that talent and skill for positively connecting with others form a basis for a powerful personal brand.

2) MAKE THE MOST OF YOUR LIFE

Are you doing something you enjoy each week? Recently, while in Hollywood, I choreographed an action scene (yes, I have a photo of my doing a martial arts move complete with the Hollywood sign on the hill—in the background). It felt like coming home. Here's how you can bring more success and joy to your life. We'll use the I.N. process:

I – Intensify
N – Nurture

1. Intensify

Too many of us get so busy that we let what we love to do just drift away. Instead, find a way to focus on what makes you glad to be alive. Find some way to engage with something creative (like I did while in Hollywood). I devote a lot of my time toward being a producer and writer (in honor of the observance of the 100th anniversary of the Titanic Disaster, I wrote a book in the genre of "alternative history/science fiction." The book is entitled *TimePulse: Beyond Titanic.* See 8 free chapters on Amazon.com).

Then, I "intensified" my life by coming back to directing an action scene choreography in the last couple of days. What a joy! It's like going swimming if you've been away from a swimming pool—and you really enjoyed swimming in earlier days.

2. Nurture

When I talk about "nurture," I'm focusing on two things:

1) take care of yourself to have more energy and 2) enrich your creative pursuit.

To do something more than going to work and then collapsing on the couch, you need energy. So get more sleep, exercise, and eat nutritious foods. Basic—yes. But essential if you want to have the capacity to do your creative pursuit.

Secondly, nurture your experience of your creative pursuit. For example, to do the action scene, I had people with me who helped me do better work—including a great actor, David MacDowell Blue, and one of my favorite camera people.

To make the most of your life, remember to dive back into some creative pursuit you love. You'll feel new energy coursing though your veins, you'll have a big smile, and people will enjoy being near you.

Some Thoughts on "Intensify" and Happiness

Do people consider you a "live wire," that is, someone who always has something interesting going on? That would be good for your personal brand. So be careful about your habitual comments. Do you think people want to talk with someone who says "Oh, just the same old thing" or "You know, same old, same old."

I advise my clients to simply sprinkle a couple of interesting tidbits in their conversations. For example, I used to wear a tie that had musical notes on it. At a networking event, someone would ask, "Can you play those notes?" And I'd reply, "I haven't tried it, but a couple of weeks ago I was at the recording studio. So how do you know our host?"

My plan was to sprinkle a detail and then return the conversation spotlight to the person by asking a question.

Often, the person would ask me about the recording studio session. I'd reply briefly and then ask another question. My principle is: "When you're listening, you're winning." That is, people love to talk about themselves, so I give them lots of opportunities.

When you "intensify" by finding a way to focus on what makes you glad to be alive, you have a new spring in your step. You radiate happiness. When that is part of your personal brand, you attract more opportunities.

3) REWARD YOURSELF WITH A SPECIAL GIFT

Imagine rewarding yourself with a special gift. Sounds fun, right? Did you think of some item to give yourself? Or perhaps an experience you long for? We'll use the C.A.N. process:

C – Cast yourself
A – Announce your intention (carefully)
N – Nurture your path

1. Cast yourself

Put yourself into some form of role that you really want. Now, that is a real gift to yourself! For example, some years ago, I wanted to direct a particular feature film. When a particular actor was unavailable, my co-producer asked, "Tom, why don't you play that role?" There were many reasons to say "No." But I cast myself anyway. And yes, the pressure of acting and directing was intense, but the adventure was worth it. Do not wait for people to say yes to you. Find some way to do what you want on a small scale. That's what I mean by cast yourself.

Do you want to act? Find a way to act. I'm delighted with how many people go into action and make short films for YouTube.com. You need to show the world what you can do. As I mentioned earlier, that's how Justin Bieber began: He posted videos of his doing cover versions of Usher's songs. Then Usher saw the videos and became the producer of songs sung by Justin! Cast yourself.

2. Announce your intention (carefully)

To make big things happen, you need to carefully announce your intention to someone who will truly support your efforts. Some friends and family members just do not believe in possibilities and in you making a big leap forward. So don't talk to them about your plans and dreams. Those particular individuals are "energy-drainers," and do not let them near your dreams.

However, other individuals could support you and help you make dreams come true. For example, when I coach graduate students in how to express an "elevator speech" (brief words about who you are), I invite them to say something like this:

"Hi, I'm Susan Ironhart. I'm currently completing a degree in animation at [school name]. I'm looking for an animator position at Pixar or Weta Digital. Ultimately, I want to direct an animated feature film. I'm best known for putting in small touches that really bring a character alive. What's one of your favorite animated films?"

The idea is to share with someone, perhaps a top person in your industry, what your ultimate goal is. Many top professionals see themselves in ambitious young people just starting out. And they "pay it forward" by serving in some way like a mentor for someone who knows what she wants and is taking steps forward.

3. Nurture your path

If you nurture a garden, you get rid of weeds, and you provide nutrients for the soil. We can apply this metaphor to your life path of making dreams come true. I began this article with the phrase: Reward Yourself with a Special Gift. A great gift for yourself is a life of adventure by taking appropriate risks. Steve Alten sold his used car and hired a great editor to work on his manuscript for his novel Meg. That's what I call nurturing your path. He nurtured his work and gained coaching to become a better writer. By the way, Meg became the first in a series of four (so far) bestselling books.

I invite you to nurture your path. Cast yourself. And consider a special gift for yourself as not just something material.

What you want is to feel good. Be sure to set up valuable experiences for yourself.

I recall an author talking about how he and his wife may not have had lots of cash to give things to their children. Instead, they made sure to provide a lot of uplifting experiences.

Give yourself the special gift of taking some steps forward on your unique, positive and hopeful path to making your dreams come true.

Some Thoughts on "Cast Yourself" and Happiness

Researchers have demonstrated that people who feel a "high internal locus of control" believe their own actions create positive events and results. "Internal" refers to inside the person, and "locus of control" refers to the person as the source of power. People who experience a high internal locus of control simply have a bit more optimism and truly get more done!

Don't wait to feel stronger. Author Marianne Williamson said, "It is easier to act your way to a new feeling than to feel your way to a new action."

Unfortunately, some people I've met have the habit of complaining about a myriad of things pushing them around, keeping them down, or holding them back. Psychologists call that having an "external locus of control."

Here's the good news: when you "cast yourself" your experience of having an internal locus of control goes up! You feel like your life is in your hands. And the truth is: You life really is in your hands. In my book *10 Seconds to Wealth,* I wrote about Divine Gifts including love, forgiveness, art, faith, grace, and humility. I also reference the idea that human beings are "co-creators" with higher power. How? We choose to a great extent what we focus on.

So while a actress, for example, is going on auditions and feeling that the producer and directors "have all the power," she can also cast herself in a short film and produce it (and then place it on YouTube.com). Now, she has something happy to talk about. She also extends her connections in the film industry. Something good will come of the process. For example, actress Felicia Day made webisodes which led directly to her getting a role on the TV show *Eureka* and performing in 13 television episodes. (More about that in my book *Darkest Secrets of the Film and Television Industry Every Actor Should Know.)*

Look for ways to cast yourself. And then your personal brand will include: "This is a proactive person."

4) HOW YOU CAN RECHARGE AND MAKE BIG THINGS HAPPEN IN YOUR LIFE

One year, a coach prompted me with the words "I want . . ." And I responded: ". . . to rest." Can you relate to that? Are you losing too much sleep? Do you feel like you're carrying the weight of the world on your shoulders? We'll use the N.O.W. process:

N – Notice
O – Open
W – Write a log

1. Notice

Ask yourself this empowering question: "Why am I so rested?"

My clients say:

- Because I exercise in the morning so it's easier to fall asleep at night
- Because I don't watch TV after 8 pm
- Because I went back to sleep in the morning—after doing some writing. (This person could do this because she usually awakens early.)

Using a question activates that part of you that automatically looks for your personal answers. So ask yourself, "Why am I so rested?" And then notice how you can modify your schedule so that you make rest a natural, non-negotiable part of your life. By "non-negotiable," I mean that you invoke some self-discipline and actually make things happen so that you get more rest. For example, at home watching a DVD with family, I have actually gotten up during the middle of the film and gone upstairs to bed. I make the decision based on a question: Is this film worth my throwing off my sleep schedule? At various times, the film is not. At other times, my family starts watching a DVD earlier in the evening so that I can keep to an empowering sleep schedule. I do admit that sometimes my sleep schedule varies.

2. Open

You need to be open to rearranging your schedule. Also, you'll need to drop some activities. Let's face it: Many of us are so busy that we become a "sleep cheat." That is, someone who cheats himself or herself of adequate sleep. I understand that you work hard and that you need some relaxation time in your life. I have discovered that when I get up early, exercise early, and have some quality alone-time in the morning, I feel better the whole day.

3. Write a log

A reliable way to change a habit is to keep a log. For example, for years, I have kept a log of how much sleep I get per night. Why? Because I place a high value on maintaining excellent health and having the capacity to do big things.

When I see that I have missed sleep for a couple of nights in a row, I do something to get more sleep.

With your log, reward yourself for doing positive activities. In this way, you become your own coach.

Start with the question: "Why am I so rested?" And then make being rested your new reality. Then you'll have more capacity to make your dreams come true.

It's worth it.

Some Thoughts on "Why am I so Rested" and Happiness

Have you noticed that many co-workers have haggard, drawn faces? Research suggests that 30% of American workers get six hours (or fewer) of sleep each night. Sleep researchers note that such little sleep fails to help people function adequately, let alone at their best.

I know that on a day when I've had less sleep, I feel the weight of the world on my shoulders. In an effort to avoid feeling out of sorts or irritable, I do something to get back into balance. Sometimes, I go to bed immediately after dinner.

A good personal brand includes calm and poise. Lack of sleep torpedoes that. So consult a doctor or sleep expert if needed. Take care of yourself, and your personal brand will be elevated.

5) WHAT FOUR WORDS WILL MAKE YOU STRONGER?

Want to take a leap forward? You'll need energy and capacity. Use this empowering question: "Does this strengthen me?" We'll use the O.N. process:

O – Open your eyes
N – Nurture yourself

1. Open your eyes

The power of the question "Does this strengthen me?" is that it can expand your vision and your awareness. Some friends or relatives may tell you, "Would you give up on that already? You've never had a big success with that ever."

A particular friend said that to me once; then he added, "I'm telling you this for your own good." I asked, "Is there anything else you need me to hear?" That was when it became clear to me that his words weren't for my own good. It just annoyed him to hear that I was still working on a particular project. His comment was just to stop something from annoying him.

The truth is that some projects or activities take time so that we grow into a new role in life. Certain people can't understand that.

So after I heard my friend out, I said, "From everything you've said, it sounds like there are a number of things I do that annoy you. So it seems like we just need some space—away from each other."

I decided at that point that talking to this person did not strengthen me. And in truly listening during the conversation, my eyes were opened to the truth. This person was not truly supporting me. His negative fortune-telling was the opposite of my colleagues who help me improve my projects, such as the editors who give me "tough love," guiding me to write better.

Remember, ask yourself: "Does this strengthen me?"

2. Nurture yourself

Let's look at this truth together: when you nurture yourself, you develop capacity. And with capacity, you can be nurturing to others.

Many of us pride ourselves on being supportive friends and family members. And that's good. And still, we must take care so that we do not overextend ourselves. People will fill up your time—if you let them. What's the solution? It's for you to focus on what you truly want so that you will be careful and thoughtful about your time and schedule.

For example, there was a time when I substantially changed my personal schedule. I discovered that if I went to sleep earlier and rose earlier, I could get in writing and exercise time before everyone in my household awakened—including the two cats.

I simply felt refreshed before interacting with anyone during the day.

Nurturing myself made a huge difference! It was like a huge weight lifted from my shoulders. This process of early to bed and early to rise—and writing and exercising in the mornings—simply brought more good feelings into my daily experience.

I invite you to find ways to nurture yourself.

One of the most useful methods is to take a break. For example, I write in the morning. When I feel fatigued, I take a break and go for a run. I return to the computer refreshed.

With more capacity, you'll feel better, and people will feel better near you, too.

When you ask yourself "Does this strengthen me?" you'll do well by cutting some activities that drain you.

When you nurture yourself, you will improve your experience of daily life.

Some Thoughts on "Does this strengthen me?" and Happiness

My work with clients has revealed that people who do not feel strong have a corresponding low feeling of happiness. Earlier I mentioned a quote from author Marianne Williamson: "It is easier to act your way to a new feeling than to feel your way to a new action." I find this distinction to have profound consequences. Start with the question "Does this strengthen me?" and then make a plan to alter your own behavior. Then take action. That's where you have true influence.

For example, I purposely talk only briefly with relatives who speak with a "poisoning tongue." Why? Because I lose time and good feelings when I have to "detox" after such an interaction. Instead, be sure to find those people who build you up. If certain family members tear you down, devote time to building wholesome friendships. Realize that people do not change until they're absolutely good and ready to—and not a moment before. So in the meantime, nurture your positive friendships. That creates good energy for all of us. And you'll simply feel happier.

6) Talk About What You Love

Do you want more energy and better relationships—both business and personal? Focus on "talk about what you love." We'll use the U.P. process:

U – Untangle yourself from habitual complaining
P – Point to what works

1. Untangle yourself from habitual complaining

How do people bond with each other? Many commiserate. What a word "commiserate." They share misery—in fact they co-operate to create more!

Instead, make a new, empowering habit: Talk about what you love, not what you hate.

What do you love in your current life?

To some, it may seem that just talking about what you love is bolstered with denying the tough parts of life. I realize that we all deal with problems and some of them are major and press us to grieve. On the other hand, many of us have been conditioned to merely complain and neglect talking about what's positive in our lives.

The truth is many of us have positive things in life like friends, family, a job, and a safe place to sleep. And we forget how these are truly blessings. Further, if you're taking daily steps toward something you like (perhaps a hobby or some entrepreneurial pursuit), then you do have something positive to talk about.

2. Point to what works

My neighbor who races motorcycles said, "You go where you're looking." That's a reason that motorcycle racers avoid looking at a wall—because they do NOT want to crash into it!

So when we talk about "point to what works"—we're talking about accentuating the positive, and then you'll continue going in that positive direction.

Many people lose too much time talking about unfair things that have happened in their past. I invite you to focus most of your energy on your present choices and opportunities. We have a choice in every moment. Recently, I read a phrase in a book: "Make peace with each moment." This means, to me, that I have a choice to cherish this present moment and not waste it on past disappointments.

Often, I find that I purposely avoid rehashing bad times or disappointments when I talk with friends. There's a whole world of opportunities out there—if we'll just look in that direction.

Don't look at the wall!

Focus and talk about what you love. You'll brighten your own day—and make a positive contribution to those around you.

Some Thoughts on "Talk About What You Love" and Happiness

To have "generally happy person" as part of your personal brand, you need to override parts of your brain. Your emotional brain is on constant lookout to avoid loss. Simultaneously, your reptile brain is focused on survival. Researchers have noted that negative details instantly go into your long-term memory. However, you must consciously focus on something positive for 10 seconds or more before it goes into your long term memory. (I talk more about this in my book *10 Seconds to Wealth*). To talk about your love helps you create those positive 10 seconds so that you know and feel what is working and going well in your life.

Let's face it: culture and conditioning keep us focused on the negative. The old phrase in journalism is: If it bleeds, it leads. And TV news broadcasts are designed to be scary enough to bring you back after the commercial. Often, there is the hook just before the commercial: "Coming up next: new computer viruses are spreading. Find out how your home computer could be crippled at this very moment." And then there is a commercial.

It just doesn't seem interesting (to TV news broadcasters, at least) that 2 billion people went home last night and hugged their family members.

So take control of your brain, your life, and your personal brand by talking about what you love.

7) Open the Door so You Feel Happy

What if you could make your life much happier? Focus on this question: "Why Am I Happy?" We'll use the O.N. process:

O – Open
N – Notice

1. Open

Imagine you could open the door to happiness even in the presence of uncertainty. That's the task. If we wait until so many loose ends are tied up, we'll miss life and happiness. Let's face it together. There is always something pending. Something "not right yet."

Our choice is to focus on the question "Why am I happy?" as opposed to "When ____ happens, then I'll be happy." There's always something that we'd prefer to have or to get done or to get past. So it's not helpful to obsess on "When ____ happens, then I'll be happy."

Now, this moment, is the real gift—and it is truly all that we have.

2. Notice

When you ask yourself "Why am I happy?" there's a part of you that automatically answers. When you ask this question, you notice what is positive in your life.

Some losses are overwhelming for a time. I remember the end of one romantic relationship. I cried and cried. Eventually, there came a time when I was able to be sad yet see some positive things still going on in my life. I still had friends, family, my health, and a direction and purpose for my life.

When we notice our blessings, something good happens. The door to gratitude can open. Trust me: When you feel gratitude, you simply feel better. It all begins with the question "Why am I happy?"

Some Thoughts on "Why Am I Happy" and Your Personal Brand

If your personal brand includes "This person is generally happy," you're likely to get more business and more cooperation. Why? People simply like to be around those who make them feel good. At the same time, it's good to avoid putting on a plastic smile. One way that I show that I'm both generally happy and that I'm a real person is to tell the truth but to also reduce the time dwelling on something negative.

For example, one day an elderly relative said some really hurtful comments in a phone conversation. One of my team members asked, "Are you okay, Tom?" I replied, "I'm bouncing back. I just had a bumpy time with a family member on the phone. But many things are going well today. So how did it go with the storyboards?"

So I acknowledged that I have personal ups and downs, but I didn't dwell on the negative moments. One tough phone call does not ruin my day. And I will ask myself, "Why am I happy?" I write down all the things that went right in my day in my personal journal every night. I have so much to be grateful for. And I know it and feel it.

8) Watch Out for Three Words that Can Get You In Trouble

What are three words that can get you into trouble? "I deserve this." Have you ever overeaten or spent too much on some item? Did "I deserve this" pop into your mind? "Hey, I deserve this . . . third piece of pie, recliner, new high-end car . . ." We'll use the D.O. process:

D – Drop demands and explore your preferences
O – Open to possibilities

1. Drop demands and explore your preferences.

I'll say it right now. You deserve all the blessings: the chocolate cake, the top level home entertainment system. All of it.

The important question is: What do you really want? Because, whatever you want, you're going to pay for it! I have a phrase "Expensive so Choose Well." Too much chocolate cake, and you "pay for it." Too many consumer purchases, and you won't have the funds for your highest priorities.

I work many hours, and I may feel that I deserve more ice cream or 327 books from Amazon.com. But what do I really want? To feel healthy and strong. What else? To feel that I'm using my various budgets in an empowering manner.

"I deserve this" is an idea that relates to demands. It's sort of similar to "I work really hard, so I demand more ice cream because I deserve this."

I suggest that you "drop demands and explore your preferences."

So the question is not about whether you deserve positive things in life. It's about whether you consciously decide what will empower you, give you value, and get you smiling.

At the moment, someone I know, "Matilda," is upset with her friend Susan. Matilda feels she knows exactly what Susan should do: get a particular graduate degree and quit her job. Really? Matilda knows this—for certain?

My point here is that both Matilda and Susan have automatic demands. Matilda, through her insistent manner, demands that Susan acknowledge that she's right. Perhaps, she would like to hear this: "You're right, Matilda. I've been wrong all along. I'll apply to XYZ Graduate School in the next 10 minutes."

Susan, however, demands that Matilda back off.

Will they get their demands met? Maybe. Maybe not.

But here's something they'll get if they both remain rigid: drama, pain, wasted time—and perhaps damage to their friendship.

How about they both convert a demand into a preference?

Susan would like to demand that Matilda "let her be" and simply "understand her."

Instead, Susan can gently express her preference and then see what happens. If Matilda stays rigid and demanding, then Susan can choose to avoid calling her at times when Susan feels vulnerable.

Meanwhile, Matilda can also switch from demanding to preferring. Matilda could prefer that Susan consider her advice, but she could also let go and trust that Susan will find her own path.

Demands, particularly with friends, cause trouble.

Expressing a preference can often help.

One of my clients recently asked, "But what happens

when you express your preference and then the other person does not respect your request?"

Sometimes, you may choose to "have some space" or "time away" from certain people. You're choosing where you'll be, and you avoid "demanding" that anyone change.

2. Open to possibilities

Recently, a friend said, "That won't work. You've never had success with that product line in the past."

Whoa, stop.

Just because something didn't work before does not guarantee that it will never work—particularly if you've learned much in the meantime and if you're getting new support and have a new plan.

It all begins with being "open to possibilities." You need to start with the idea that something you want is possible. How does this relate to "I deserve this"?

"I deserve this" gets us into trouble because we're focusing solely on "this." And as we focus on the "this," we're demanding that "this" happens only in the way we want it to. It's like walking with blinders on.

Sure, I prefer that all my books become best-sellers. But that's a preference.

There are many good things related to my writing 23 books. For example, in writing the books, I have thought deeply on a variety of topics. I like ideas and learning, and I've grown as a human being.

I get emails from people who tell me of the value they've gained from the books, and that brightens my day. It feels great to be helpful to others. (Free chapters of the books are visible at Amazon.com.)

And another benefit is that a number of people read my books and then want to partner with me on business opportunities. Why? Because they have learned of my experiences and my understanding.

I invite you to take the blinders off, start expressing preferences, and see what surprise-blessings blossom in your life.

Remember, it's not about "I deserve this."

You're a worthwhile person; you already deserve blessings.

It's really about consciously deciding to take action for what you really want.

Some Thoughts on "I Deserve This" and Happiness

Some people, as they become successful, also become significantly impatient and irritable. That does *not* form an effective personal brand. I support that a professional can be "demanding" as in requiring people to fulfill their promises and vigorous deadlines. But the attitude of "I deserve this because I'm special" can get anyone into some significant trouble. It causes resentment, and one starts to get poor service as people, sometimes subconsciously, are demotivated to do their best.

So how do we avoid going overboard with the "demanding approach"? Have someone you trust observe your behavior and then have a "post-game" conversation—by that I mean, after the interaction, have a *post-interaction* discussion. Be open to valid coaching. You can be both a "demanding" client and a positive person. For example, a vendor recently kept me waiting. I've known this person for years and have brought a lot of my business to him. I said that I felt bothered and *I did not want this to be a trend.* I was careful to avoid expressing my frustration with any harsh words. He made up for his error by extending some extra service. And I thanked him and have not brought up the incident again. There was no need. I protected my time and also protected this important business relationship.

9) Protect Your Time and Find New Energy

Would you like more energy? Then, you'll have to protect your time. We'll use the U.P. process:

U – Untangle
P – Purpose your time

1. Untangle

At one point, I was invited to travel to another state. Some friends "Jonathan" and "Sheryl" invited my sweetheart and me to stay at their home. But one day, I was talking with my coach, and I discovered something powerful. I could not relax with the people who had invited me. Why? They had so many "rules." It was their home, and I fully support people being comfortable in their own home. However, their "rules" made me uncomfortable. Have you ever worked with or lived with someone who could be called a "control freak"? No relaxation there.

So I did something difficult. I personally declined going to that particular home [I "untangled" myself]. My sweetheart went ahead and visited with Jonathan and Sheryl. That was fine. We're not joined at the hip.

I devote much of my life to service—to listening to clients, friends and family members. That takes energy. Sometimes I feel depleted. If I'm going to recharge my batteries, I'm going to have to be careful with my choices. I coined a phrase "Expensive so choose well." What I mean by that is this: my leisure time is in such short supply that, to me, it is expensive. If I choose to share my leisure time with someone, I want to make sure that the interaction does not drain my energy.

Now, let's pause for a moment. We all have uncomfortable times—perhaps with some family members. We have family obligations, and we need to be supportive to family members. I call that "family time." On the other hand, when I'm talking about "untangle," I'm referring to your true leisure time. Choose well.

2. Purpose your time

Many of us have heard about "repurposing" something. Perhaps you wrote an article, and you can "repurpose" it to be a speech for an association. Along these lines, let's talk about "purpose your time." What is the purpose for your activity? Do you anticipate having a good time?

So to "purpose your time," ask yourself: "Does this activity drain me or refresh me?"

When I asked myself this question, I thought, "I want to talk to people who are full of hope and life, people who are making good things happen." So I decided to "purpose my time" and avoid spending time with certain "downer people."

This reminds me of Louise Hay's comment: "I'm no longer curious about things that upset me."

Be good to yourself. Protect your energy, and you'll likely be kinder to people near you.

That is a blessing.

Some Thoughts on "Protecting Your Time" and Happiness

If you feel that you don't have any time to yourself, you likely feel overburdened. I realize that we're all so busy. So I suggest you become "time strategic." Find little pockets of time to use as you prefer. Among my friends, I'm well known for always having a book with me. Why? I never know when there will be a delay. Let's say a friend suddenly has to negotiate with a vendor, and I'm not needed. I don't get upset about the delay: I have a book with me. It's not wasted time when I have a book. I enjoy constantly learning and pondering new ideas and data that I come across.

Even a mere ten minutes of soaking in a hot bath can truly brighten your day. I have a phrase "Better than Zero." My clients often find that a regular amount of relaxation and time away from work helps them—even if that time comes in short durations.

So be sure to take breaks. You'll find that you'll have more moments of feeling happy. And you'll discover that people feel comfortable near you—and that supports a positive personal brand.

10) Free Up Your Energy and Get More Done

Would you like more energy to make each new year phenomenal? I'll now share with you a powerful method that begins with three words: "It's just stuff." And, we'll use the I.T. process.

I – identify
T – target

1. Identify

You need to identify what is truly vital for your happiness. The technique of saying to yourself "It's just stuff" is a shortcut to an attitude called "non-attachment." For example, I experienced twinges of sadness with the closing of Borders bookstores. Why? I had enjoyed many times exploring and finding new books. A Borders store was a place for me to relax and have fun, because I read a lot of books (85 books in 2013).

I've learned to avoid wallowing in sad feelings. To quickly move onto a new feeling and new energy, I tell myself "It's just stuff." This phrase (which is an example of what I call a "Switch Phrase") switches the direction of my thoughts. By saying "it's just stuff," I remind myself that I have other ways to have fun—like calling up a friend and having a conversation. You see, I have just reminded myself that material objects are not the only way to enjoy life.

The idea of "non-attachment" relates to being free to think other things and have other feelings. On the other hand, I know people who are truly attached to some things, and it just creates misery. We can be attached to physical things like jewelry or books – you name it.

We also get attached to ideas. For example, if Sam says, "I can't be happy if my mother keeps criticizing me"—then Sam is attached to an idea. This is a problem because his mother may never approve of him or his actions.

On the other hand, *Approval is an occasional dessert*. This idea occurred to me when I noticed that some extended family members tend to be hyper-critical. Over the years, I have taught myself not to "demand" or expect approval from various people. I have identified that someone's approval is not required for me to have an enjoyable life. I can even say, metaphorically, that someone's lack of approval is "just stuff"—and I can flow onward with my life.

2. Target

Many of us have career goals. We might call them targets. But I'm going to add having good feelings now as another form of a target.

Let's say your target is to have better relationships. You can use two phrases on a daily basis: 1) "it's just stuff" and 2) "make space for people to feel their feelings." When some troublesome moments come up with a friend or family member, repeat one of these phrases silently to yourself.

Above, I've talked about the idea of being non-attached. Imagine that you can figure out what "stuff" you can drop (what you can be non-attached to). For example, in my wide circle of friends, some friends tend to argue with each other. I've learned to drop the "stuff" of trying to broker peace between them.

I've also learned to "make space for people to feel their feelings." For example, I have a friend "George" who is a vegetarian and he wants a $1.00 discount when he orders a dish and wants chicken or red meat left out of the meal. I remind myself to "make space for people to feel their feelings." George feels that he has a right to push for certain changes. Okay. I also hold an idea: "People can ask for what they want." My point is that I do not expect or demand that George change. I drop "the stuff."

Also, I do not expect or demand that I'll always have the patience to be near George's big "$1.00 negotiation" at the restaurant table. Sometimes, I choose to decline going to a restaurant with George.

I make space for other people to have their feelings. And I make space for me to have my feelings.

And guess what?

I feel free.

This is the power of non-attachment.

By the way, you and I can choose what to be attached to. I am attached to the idea of being kind to my friends and family. I am attached to doing my best to demonstrate loving actions toward loved ones.

And I identify what I can let go of.

In this way, I free up a lot of energy. I can use this energy to be really productive.

I invite you to:

- Identify what is truly vital for your happiness. (Let go of other things.)
- Target the good experiences you want in your life. (Let go of things that do not help you.)

Some Thoughts on "It's Just Stuff," Happiness and Your Personal Brand

Some people cringe when near anyone they label a "control freak" or oversensitive. Do you know someone who seems to make a big thing out of any minor disappointment? Do you find yourself going out of your way to avoid a control freak? Let's face it, "control freak" does not make an effective personal brand. It's better to be known as "tough but fair" or "demanding excellence but not neurotic."

How do you avoid that "control freak" label? Practice non-attachment and let go. Begin with telling yourself "it's just stuff." You'll enjoy more moments of calm. Here's another helpful idea:

If you can solve a problem with money, it is not a problem. It's an expense. — Harvey Mackay

This quote suggests that when you have a course of action, you can move forward and experience less unease. This quote invites us to change our mindset. Instead of feeling the stress of a problem, we think of our solution as an investment to make things better. For example, I do *not* go with the lowest price web host for my multiple websites. Why? Because I use two companies that have been absolutely reliable for years. On the other hand, I have colleagues who have complained bitterly about their websites going down. So I have, as Harvey noted in his quote, "solved a problem with money." That is, I invest a bit more money so that I have the freedom to focus on my projects and avoid losing any time with concerns about web hosts.

My point here is to make good choices, and they may

require that you invest in your health and happiness. Here's another example about investing our money in solutions. Recently, a friend narrowly missed being pummeled when two branches fell off a tree on the property where he lives. The owners of the condominium complex delayed for five days in getting a dangerous tree removed because they were waiting for three estimates to get a low price for removing the huge cedar tree. The tree's remaining branches hung over a neighbor's house. Personally, I would have paid more money and gone with a reliable, although a bit more expensive, company that could get the job done *the next day.* Basically, the owners decided to play Russian Roulette for five days. Any of those days, the other branches could have tumbled down on the neighbor's house killing people or damaging property. And an added problem could have been a resulting lawsuit.

More money can be earned, which means money is replaceable. But taking chances with lives and property damage strikes me as unwise.

In summary, we talked about making good choices and these relate to having an effective personal brand. A powerful personal brand includes "decisive" and "has good priorities" and "willing to invest in solutions—with good timing."

A FINAL WORD AND THE SPRINGBOARD TO YOUR DREAMS

Congratulations on your efforts with this book.

Our dinner gathering featuring the insights of the seven notable people is coming to a close. Here are a few more gems of wisdom.

Be thankful for what you have; you'll end up having more. If you concentrate on what you don't have, you will never, ever have enough. - Oprah Winfrey

All of our notable guests pointed out that loving what you do is important.

Your work is going to fill a large part of your life, and the only way to be truly satisfied is to do what you believe is great work. And the only way to do great work is to love what you do. If you haven't found it yet, keep looking. Don't settle. As with all matters of the heart, you'll know when you find it. - Steve Jobs

We make the kind of movies we like to watch. I love to laugh. I love to be amazed by how beautiful it is. But I also love to be moved to tears. There's lots of heart in our films. - John Lasseter

Helen Keller pointed out that optimism is necessary to excel. She said, *"Optimism is the faith that leads to achievement. Nothing can be done without hope and confidence."*

Martin Luther King, Jr. invited us all to keep stepping forward. He said, *"Faith is taking the first step even when you don't see the whole staircase."*

As the evening ended, Oprah brought a smile to us all as she said, "I still have my feet on the ground, I just wear better shoes."

* * *

As we come to the close of this book, I'm grateful to have had the opportunity to share insights with you.

In this book, we have covered *countermeasures* to the tough situations in business communication.

You have learned to create your effective personal brand.

To gain more value from this book, be sure to go through it and develop your own To Do List. Take some action. Any action towards improving skills and promoting yourself is helpful. I often say, "Better than zero."

Please consider gaining special training through my coaching (phone and in-person), workshops, presentations and Top Five Group Elite Video Training.

As you continue to work toward expanding your

financial abundance, you are likely to come up against some tough situations. To be supportive I've written a number of books . . .

- Darkest Secrets of Charisma
- Darkest Secrets of Persuasion and Seduction Masters: How to Protect Yourself and Turn the Power to Good
- Darkest Secrets of Negotiation Masters
- Darkest Secrets of Making a Pitch to the Film and Television Industry
- Darkest Secrets of Film Directing
- Darkest Secrets of the Film and Television Industry Every Actor Should Know
- Darkest Secrets of Spiritual Seduction Masters
- Success Secrets of Rich, Smart and Powerful People: How You Can Use Leverage for Business Success

See my blog at
www.BeHeardandBeTrusted.com

The best to you and may you continue to change the world,

Tom
Tom Marcoux,
America's Communication Coach
Motion Picture Director, Actor, Producer, Screenwriter
P.S. See **Free Chapters** of Tom Marcoux's 23 books
at http://amzn.to/ZiCTRj

Titles include:
Be Heard and Be Trusted
Nothing Can Stop You This Year
Truth No One Will Tell You

10 Seconds to Wealth
Your Secret Charisma
Wake Up Your Spirit to Prosperity
The Cat Advantage
— and more.
(For coaching, reach Tom Marcoux
at tomsupercoach@gmail.com)

EXCERPT FROM *DARKEST SECRETS OF PERSUASION AND SEDUCTION MASTERS: HOW TO PROTECT YOURSELF AND TURN THE POWER TO GOOD*

by Tom Marcoux, America's Communication Coach
Copyright Tom Marcoux

. . . Now, I am in my 40's, with gray in my hair, and for 27 years I have been taking action to protect people.

And now is the time for me to protect you with the Countermeasures I reveal in this book.

Every human being needs to be able to
break the trance that a Manipulator creates.
You need to make good decisions
so you are safe and you keep growing
—and you are not cut down and crippled.

This Secrets material is so intense that I first released it only with the counterbalance of my most energizing and uplifting books, *Nothing Can Stop You This Year!* and *10 Seconds to Wealth: Master the Moment Using Your Divine Gifts.*

An interviewer asked me: "Who can be the Manipulator?"

A co-worker, a boss, a salesperson, someone you're dating, and someone you think is a friend.

Now is the time—this very minute—for me to write this book to protect you.

I must speak the truth.

These Darkest Secrets of "persuasion masters" are ...

Wait a minute! Let's say it plainly: These are the Darkest Secrets of masters of manipulation. Throughout this book, I will call these people what they are: Manipulators.

Dictionary.com defines "manipulate" as "To influence or manage shrewdly or deviously.... To tamper with or falsify for personal gain."

In this book, we will look on a manipulator as one who deviously influences someone with no concern about that person's well-being, and who causes harm to that person.

Here is the first Darkest Secret:

Darkest Secret #1:
Manipulators Make You Hurt
and Then Offer the Salve.

Manipulators would invite you to go out in the sun for hours and then sell you the salve to soothe your burns. The problem is that we don't notice that this is what they're doing.

For example, you're considering the purchase of a house. A Manipulator asks the question, "So, where would you put your TV?" This question is designed to put you into a trance.

Dictionary.com defines "trance" as "a half-conscious state, seemingly between sleeping and waking, in which ability to function voluntarily may be suspended." Let's condense this: in a trance you may not be able to function freely.

Here is the second Secret:

Darkest Secret #2:
Manipulators Put You into a Trance.

To protect yourself, you must learn to use Countermeasures to Break the Trance.

All the Countermeasures (actions you can take to break the trance) in this book will make you stronger and more capable of protecting yourself.

Now, we'll view the third Secret:

Darkest Secret #3:

Manipulators Care Nothing for You and Human Decency:

They'll lie, cheat, and do whatever they need to do so they win—but their charm masks all this.

Let's return to the example of a Manipulator selling you a house. A Manipulator does not pause for an instant to see if you can truly afford the new house. The Manipulator would neglect to mention that you will not only have your mortgage payment of $900. There will be additional costs: home repairs, property tax, water, electricity, homeowner's insurance, and more. The Manipulator only emphasizes what he or she knows you want to hear: "Look! $900 is better than the $1500 you're paying for rent, which is just going down the toilet. And the $900 is an investment."

Let's go back to **Secret #1:**

Manipulators make you hurt and then offer the salve.

The Manipulator has you feeling good about the solution (salve) and feeling bad about your current life situation.

How? A Manipulator will make you hurt through questions such as:

• What bothers you about paying $1500 a month for rent? (The Manipulator will use a derisive tone when he says the word rent.)

• What is not smart about paying rent on someone else's house instead of investing in your own house?

• How do you feel about your children walking in the neighborhood where you live now?

Do you see how these questions are designed to make you hurt enough so that you'll buy?

An interviewer asked me, "Tom, aren't these good arguments for purchasing a house?"

"What we're looking at is the *intention* of the influencer," I replied. "Let's look at our definition of a manipulator as one who deviously influences someone with no concern about that person's well-being, and who causes harm to that person. If the person truly cannot afford the house, he or she will be harmed by buying it. If the manipulator conceals the truth, the manipulator is doing harm. That's the important difference."

Some friends of mine are ethical and helpful real estate agents who truthfully reveal the whole situation and help the purchaser achieve her own goals.

In this book, we are talking about another type of person; that is, unethical Manipulators.

* * *

In any given moment, we need to remember the tactics

Manipulators use. We will focus on the word D.A.R.K. so you can remember details easily and protect yourself from Manipulators.

D — Dangle something for nothing
A — Alert to scarcity
R — Reveal the Desperate Hot Button
K — Keep on pushing buttons

1. Dangle Something for Nothing

What do conmen and conwomen do to seize your attention? They make you think you're getting a "steal."

I recently saw a documentary in which a conman on a street in England showed a toy that looked like it was dancing. This fake product was actually dancing because of a hidden, invisible thread. The conman was dangling something for nothing. The Entranced Buyer thought he was getting something worth $20 for only $5. That was the trick. The Entranced Buyer felt that he was getting $15 extra of value for his $5. What the Buyer really got was something worth nothing. Similarly, I know someone who purchased a copy of a Disney movie from a street vendor in San Francisco. She brought the copy home and it was unwatchable—and the street vendor was never seen again.

An old phrase goes, "A conman cannot con someone who is not looking for something for nothing."

How to Protect Yourself from "Dangle Something for Nothing"

Stop! Get on your cell phone and talk through the "deal" with someone you know who thinks clearly. Go home. Think about it. Do some research on the Internet. Listen to your gut feelings. If the salesman or conman is too insistent, get away from that Manipulator. Get quiet. Have a cup of water. Cool down. Break the Trance!

Break the Trance and Identify the Crucial Detail

Earlier, I mentioned that a Manipulator puts you into a trance. An added problem is that we put ourselves into a trance. For example, as you read this, are you thinking about your right toe? Most likely not (unless you stubbed your toe recently). The point is that we only focus on a tiny percentage of what is going on in our life.

Around fifteen years ago, I caused myself trouble because I put myself into a trance. I discovered that under certain conditions, friendship can make you nearly deaf. Here's how: I was producing a song for a motion picture. A good friend was singing backup in the chorus. Because of our friendship, I wanted him to sound great. I completely missed the Crucial Detail. In this kind of situation, the Crucial Detail is that what truly counts is how the lead singer sounds! I made a song that I could not release. What a waste of time and money! I had put myself into a trance.

In any situation in which the Manipulator is "dangling something for nothing," we often fall into a trance and miss the Crucial Detail. The most important detail is *not* that we're saving money if we order before midnight tonight. What counts is whether the product creates a lasting, crucial benefit in our lives. And is the benefit of the product worth the cost? Some people even program themselves to make mistakes by saying, "I can't pass up a bargain." The bargain is *not* the Crucial Detail.

Secrets to Break the Trance

This is the process of B.R.E.A.K.S. It will help you remember the proven methods to break a trance.

B — Breathe
R — Relax
E — Envision
A — Act on aromas
K — Keep moving
S — Smile

Secret #1: Breathe

Remember Secret #1: Manipulators make you hurt and then offer the salve. The Manipulator wants to put you into a state of being that fills you with a sense of urgency and anxiety. Oh, no! I'm going to miss the sale!

Stop this highly vulnerable state. Take a deep breath. Do it now. Take a deep breath and let your belly "get fat" by filling it with air. As you breathe out, let your belly deflate. Breathe in through your nose and breathe out through your mouth. This is called belly-breathing. Repeat the actions of belly-breathing three times. Good. Now, do you feel different? Remember, when you are relaxed, you are strong.

End of Excerpt from
DARKEST SECRETS OF PERSUASION AND SEDUCTION MASTERS: HOW TO PROTECT YOURSELF AND TURN THE POWER TO GOOD

Purchase your copy of this book (paperback or ebook) at Amazon.com or BarnesandNoble.com

See **Free Chapters** of Tom Marcoux's 23 books at http://amzn.to/ZiCTRj

ABOUT THE AUTHOR

Tom Marcoux helps people like you fulfill big dreams. Known as America's Communication Coach, Tom has authored 22 books with sales in 15 countries. One of his *Darkest Secrets* books rose to #1 on Amazon.com Hot New Releases in Business Life (and in Business Communication). He guides clients and audiences (IBM, Sun Microsystems, etc.) to success in job interviewing, public speaking, media relations, and branding. A member of the National Speakers Association, he is a professional coach and guest expert on TV, radio, and print, and was dubbed "the Personal Branding Instructor" by the *San Francisco Examiner.* Tom addressed National Association of Broadcasters' Conference six years running. With a degree in psychology, Tom is a guest lecturer at **Stanford University**, DeAnza, & California State University, and teaches public speaking, science fiction cinema/literature and comparative religion at Academy of Art University. Winner of a special award at the **Emmys**, Tom wrote, directed, and produced a feature film that the distributor took to the **Cannes film market**, and the film gained international distribution. He is engaged in book/film projects *Crystal Pegasus* (children's) and *TimePulse* (science fiction). See TomSuperCoach.com and Tom's well-received blog at www.BeHeardandBeTrusted.com

Tom Marcoux can help you with **speech writing** and **coaching for your best performance.**

As Tom says, *Make Your Speech a Pleasant Beach.*

Join Tom's Linkedin.com group: *Executive Public Speaking and Communication Power.*

Get a **Free** report: "9 Deadly Mistakes to Avoid for Your Next Speech and 9 Surefire Methods" at http://tomsupercoach.com/freereport9Mistakes4Speech.html

Tom Marcoux has trained CEOs, small business owners, and graduate students to speak with impact and gain audiences' tremendous approval and cooperation. *Learn how to present and get thunderous applause!*

"Tom, Thanks for your coaching and work with me on revising my speech at a major university. Working with you has been so enlightening for me. Through your gentle prodding and guidance I was able to write a speech that connects with the audience. I wish everyone could experience the transformation I have undergone. You have helped me discover the warm and compelling stories that now make my speech reach hearts and uplift minds. This was truly an empowering experience. I cannot thank you enough for your great assistance." — J.S.

Become a fan of Tom's graphic novels/feature films:

Science fiction: *TimePulse*
www.facebook.com/timepulsegraphicnovel

Fantasy Thriller: *Jack AngelSword*
type "JackAngelSword" at Facebook.com

Children's Fantasy: *Crystal Pegasus*
www.facebook.com/crystalpegasusandrose

See **Free Chapters** of Tom Marcoux's 22 books
at http://amzn.to/ZiCTRj

Special Offer Just for Readers of this Book:

Contact Tom Marcoux at tomsupercoach@gmail.com for special discounts on books, coaching, workshops and presentations. Just mention your experience with this book.

ramcontent.com/pod-product-compliance
Source LLC
burg PA
0535210326
B00014B/3224